CORPORATE GOVERNANCE AT THE CROSSROADS

CORPORATE GOVERNANCE AT THE CROSSROADS

A report by
Marleen Willekens and Piet Sercu,

holders of the PwC Chair "Value and Risk"
at FETEW K.U.Leuven, 2000/01-2003/04

With editorial assistance by Kurt Desender, K.U.Leuven

intersentia
Antwerpen – Oxford

Distribution for the UK:
Hart Publishing
Salter's Boat Yard
Folly Bridge
Abingdon Road
Oxford OX1 4LB
UK
Tel: + 44 1865 24 55 33
Fax: + 44 1865 79 48 82

Distribution for North America:
Gaunt Inc.
Gaunt Building
3011 Gulf Drive
Holmes Beach
Florida 34217-2199
USA
Tel: + 1 941 778 5211
Fax: + 1 941 778 5252

Distribution for Switzerland and Germany:
Schulthess Verlag
Zwingliplatz 2
CH-8022 Zürich
Switzerland
Tel: + 41 1 251 93 36
Fax: + 41 1 261 63 94

Distribution for other countries:
Intersentia Publishers
Groenstraat 31
2640 Mortsel
Belgium
Tel: + 32 3 680 15 50
Fax: + 32 3 658 71 21

Corporate Governance at the Crossroads
Marleen Willekens and Piet Sercu

ISBN 90-5095-469-3
D/2005/7849/44
NUR 782-786

To our parents, for helping and encouraging us in our path into academia. To our partners, for their continued interest and support in spite of everything. To our offspring, for their broadminded tolerance towards the kind of stuff we write. And to Robert Peirce, Robert Roksnoer, Eddy Schuermans and Peter Van den Eynde who, as PwC members of the steering committee of the PwC Chair "Value and Risk" at K.U.Leuven, have put us up to all this.

TABLE OF CONTENTS

INTRODUCTION TO THE KU LEUVEN PWC CHAIR'S CORPORATE GOVERNANCE REPORT

PIET SERCU

BACKGROUND TO THE ROUND-TABLE DISCUSSIONS

In the fall of 1999, my colleague Marleen Willekens came to see me about a possible Research Chair at K.U. Leuven's Business Studies Department (DTEW). The Chair was to be funded, for three years, by PricewaterhouseCoopers, with whom Marleen, being professor of auditing, had excellent relations. Still, she felt, two professors taken together should generate more than twice the number & quality of ideas that one academic might have begotten on his/her own; and with me on board there would also be more of a balance in the Chair's steering committee, to which PwC was sending three people, initially.

I liked the idea (and the research money), so the five of us quickly came to an agreement. On the PwC side we had Eddy Schuermans, Peter Van den Eynde and, until his retirement, Robert Roksnoer, later replaced by Robert Peirce. In the first and second year we organized some notable seminars, featuring luminaries like John Hegarty from the FEE and the World Bank, Berkeley's Hal Varian or Shell HQ's CFO, Steve Hodge. We also organized a survey among analysts, portfolio managers and credit analysts, on the relevance of financial reports and the desirability of various conceivable changes in corporate reporting. The resulting report was published in the *Tijdschrift voor Economie en Management*, our Faculty's home journal. Next we set up panel debates: one on risk management and a second (unexpectedly vivid) one on the role of analysts and accountants in the stock-market bubble & crash. Peter and Marleen then came up with the excellent idea to study voluntary disclosure in Belgium, via annual reports and websites, and with a little help from the students in Marleen's Auditing Seminar. This led to one more PwC Chair seminar as well as a report, enclosed as Chapter 6 of the present book and of which an early version was published in *Accountancy en Bedrijfskunde*.

Nobody quite remembers who came up with the idea for a series of round-table discussions, to be held in the Chair's third and final year, on the corporate-governance issues raised by the familiar fraud cases. I tend to think the idea grew slowly, with valuable contributions from all five partners. There were to be five round-table meetings in total, one with representatives from various Boards of Directors, the second one with CEOs, the third with capital providers (banks, mutual funds and pension funds, insurance companies, and holding companies), the fourth with accountants and auditors, and lastly a session with academics. We sincerely thank the three K.U. Leuven colleagues who agreed to chair one session each, besides the ones chaired by Marleen and me: Stan Beckers, then Chief Investment Officer at WestLB; Herman Daems, CEO at the Flanders Regional Investment Corporation (GIMV) and Chairman of *e.g.* Barco; and Cynthia Van Hulle, also a member of many Boards and an expert on corporate-governance issues. We equally thank the many participants who, undaunted by Hail, Blizzards, and Traffic Jams agreed to spend an entire afternoon in the *Convent van Chievres* and who kept amazing us with their continuous outpouring of new views, novel ideas, and fresh facts. It was a great experience. We lastly thank Kurt Desender, hired by the Chair after the sessions, who patiently typed up the discussions, translated the Dutch-language ones into English, and wrote the first draft for Chapters 1-5. He did a super job and was promptly re-hired for a longer research project.

Towards the participants we seize the opportunity to apologize for being slowish with the final polishing stage for the book that we had promised them. Here are their names (in alphabetical order):

- *Board members*: Prof. Cynthia Van Hulle (Chair); Baron Karel Boone, Ferdinand Chaffart, Françcois Gillet, Prof. Herwig Langohr, Gerard Van Acker, Prof. Lutgart Van den Berghe, Robert van Oordt, Baron Piet van Waeyenberge; KU Leuven: Profs Piet Sercu and Marleen Willekens; PwC: Eddy Schuermans, Peter Van den Eynde;
- *CEOs*: Prof. Herman Daems (Chair); Luc Bertrand (CEO Ackermans & van Haaren), Patrick De Groote (CEO Zenitel), Herbert De Loose (CFO Duvel Moortgat), Florent Gijbels (CEO Kinepolis), Jacques Lévy-Morelle (Secretary-General Solvay, L'Institut des Administrateurs), Luc Missorten (CFO Interbrew), Kurt Moons (CEO Brantano), Luc Pintens (CEO Econocom Belgium), Annemie Reydams (CFO Neuhaus), Ajit Shetty (CEO Janssen Pharmaceutica), Henri Van Dierdonck (CEO Associated Weavers), Tonny Van Doorslaer (CEO Spector Photo Group), Martine Verluyten (CFO Mobistar), Karel Vinck (CEO NMBS); KU Leuven: Profs Piet Sercu and Marleen Willekens; PwC: Eddy Schuermans, Peter Van den Eynde;
- *Capital providers*: Prof. Stan Beckers (Chair); Peter De Coensel (Swiss Life Asset Management Belgium), Prof. William De Vijlder (Fortis Investment Management, R.U.Gent), Prof. Stefan Duchateau (KBC Asset Management, BVICB, EHSAL),

Charles Demoulin (Deminor), Jos Peeters (Quest for Growth), Karel Stroobants (BVPF), Prof. Luc Van Liedekerke (Ethibel, K.U.Leuven), Ferdinand Verdonck (Almanij), Michel Vermaerke (Belgacom, European Council on Corporate Governance and Board Effectiveness); KU Leuven: Profs Piet Sercu and Marleen Willekens; PwC: Peter Van den Eynde;
- *Accountants and Auditors*: Prof. Marleen Willekens (Chair); Pierre Berger (KPMG, Secretaris-Penningmeester IBR), Inge Boets (Ernst & Young), Prof. Joël Branson (Horwath, Vrije Universiteit Brussel), Eddy Dams (PricewaterhouseCoopers), Paul De Weerdt (PKF, Van der Steen, Riské, De Weerdt, Lefebvre & Partners), Andre Kilesse (BDO, Ondervoorzitter IBR), Prof. Robert Knechel (University of Florida, Ernst & Young), Rik Neckebroeck (Deloitte & Touche), Ludo Swolfs (Ernst & Young, Voorzitter IBR), Mark Torfs (Deloitte & Touche), Peter Van den Eynde (PricewaterhouseCoopers), Hugo Van Passel (Van Passel, Mazars & Guerard; IBR); KU Leuven: Prof Piet Sercu; PwC: Eddy Dams, Peter Van den Eynde;
- *Academics*: Prof. Piet Sercu (Chair); Professor Joël Branson (Free University of Brussels VUB, BE), Professor Willem Buijink (Tilburg University, NL), Professor Ann Gaeremynck (Leuven University, BE), Professor Grégoire Jakhian (Free University of Brussels ULB, BE), Professor Robert Knechel (University of Florida, U.S.), Professor Peter Moizer (University of Leeds, UK), Professor Ken Peasnell (University of Lancaster, UK), Professor Lutgart Van den Berghe (Vlerick Leuven Gent Management School, BE), Professor Charles Van Wymeersch (University of Namur, BE); KU Leuven: Profs Piet Sercu and Marleen Willekens; PwC: Eddy Dams, Peter Van den Eynde

Again, sincere thanks to all.

THE ROUND-TABLE DISCUSSIONS AND THEIR WRITE-UPS

The meetings themselves lasted about three hours each (not including the informal discussions over drinks, afterwards), and all followed the same format. We opened by inviting the day's panel to fill out a questionnaire on five topics: boards, audit committee, internal and external audit, and voluntary disclosure. The initial idea was to get our guests' brains ticking and to loosen them up for the debates; but we soon realised that the answers were interesting in their own right, so that the questionnaire results are now included in this book. The report below follows the same order as these questionnaires. So did the debates themselves, with the day's chair sequentially bringing up the questionnaire statements and soliciting comments from the *corona*. The discussions never fell flat, thanks to the skills of the session chairs and the interest of the participants. Everything was tape-recorded, or nearly everything: changing the tapes always made us lose a minute or two. In typing up the discussions we of course had to abbreviate, cull, and stylize. Abject apologies are in order to the participants if and when we occasionally missed a *nuance* or a bright insight. In the write-up, we decided not to identify the speakers by name, not even ourselves (a painful experience), but most of the time we do mention whether the opinion originated from a board member, a CEO, and so on.

Each of the first five chapters below deals with one of the topics in the questionnaire. A chapter always opens with a review of the academic literature on the issue at hand. Like all reviews it is necessarily incomplete, and we apologize to colleagues whose work was inadvertently overlooked. The report on the round-table discussion then follows. To set the scene for the discussion, we also provide some data that tell us how Belgian companies deal with the issue at hand, as far as we can tell from the financial statements of 2000 and 2003.

We enjoyed the meetings, the ideas, the debates, and even the writing stage. We do hope we have been able to convey some of the atmosphere to the reader, but that is perhaps easier said than done. Enjoy!

Leuven, April 2005

PREFACE CHAPTER

The wave of corporate reporting scandals (Enron, Parmalat, Ahold, ...) has worldwide triggered increased attention towards corporate transparency and the development of institutional mechanisms to enhance, stimulate and improve such transparency. In the aftermath of the scandals, policymakers and regulators on both sides of the Atlantic judged that the scandals are responsible for undermining public trust in capital markets and that regulatory intervention was necessary to restore that trust. Remarkable is that the new rules and guidelines that have emerged so far in post-Enron times mainly relate to corporate governance and external auditing issues, and much less to a direct reform of actual corporate disclosure requirements related to performance. Examples of such initiatives by policymakers include, amongst many others, the Sarbanes-Oxley Act in the US, the 2003 Action Plan on "Modernising Company Law and Enhancing Corporate Governance" at EU level, and the Corporate Governance Act 2002 and Code of Best Practice 2004 in Belgium.

Given that governance-related rules and guidelines are introduced to enhance transparency, a relevant question is whether corporate governance is indeed effective in that respect. In this book we address this question by reviewing – for each of the four mechanisms that we study (board of directors, audit committee, internal control and audit, external audit) – what the empirical literature has been reporting regarding the effectiveness of these mechanisms. Although many of the findings stem from Anglo-Saxon environments, we believe that they can provide relevant insights for policymakers outside the Anglo-Saxon world. Agency problems indeed often differ between institutional environments, and so does ownership structure. However, the Anglo-Saxon world consist of a more heterogeneous set of companies, from diversely held to concentrated, and therefore findings from the Anglo-Saxon countries are relevant and informative for non Anglo-Saxon environments.

Next to reviewing the literature to identify what the evidence is regarding the effectiveness of various governance mechanisms and characteristics, we also took stock of contemporary governance practice in Belgian listed companies. In addition we also report on a debate that we held on "restoring public trust" through a series of round-table sessions (see also introduction). At the sessions we also distributed a questionnaire probing for the opinions of round-table participants regarding certain governance practices. We report on these results as well.

So, in a nut shell, in this book we zoom in on two themes: corporate governance and corporate transparency. The governance mechanisms that we address in detail include: the board of directors (chapter 1), the audit committee (chapter 2), internal control and the internal audit function (chapter 3) and external auditing (chapter 4). The relevance of these mechanisms is apparent from contemporary corporate governance best practice codes and literature in this area. We also dedicate considerable attention to corporate transparency (chapters 5 and 6). Note that we define and measure transparency through an index which is derived from the ValueReporting™ framework developed by PricewaterhouseCoopers. In a final chapter (chapter 7) we focus on the recently introduced Belgian corporate governance code and compare the guidelines and provisions in this code with the conclusions in this study regarding the effectiveness of various governance mechanisms. In particular, we also elaborate on the evidence regarding the effectiveness of certain governance mechanisms from Belgian studies.

CHAPTER 1
THE BOARD OF DIRECTORS

The board of directors is the primary mechanism for achieving top-level separation of the management and control functions. The board receives its authority for internal control from stockholders of corporations, and its job is to hire, fire, compensate, and advise top management on behalf of those shareholders (Jensen, 1993). This delegation occurs because stockholders generally hold small stakes and, therefore, do not have a sufficiently large incentive to devote resources to ensure that management is acting in the stockholders' interest. Fama and Jensen (1983) posit that the board of directors is the prime internal control mechanism responsible for monitoring the actions of top management.

Two characteristics of the board of directors stand out in the empirical literature as being of the greatest interest for effective corporate governance: board size and independence of the board members. With respect to size, the hypothesis tested has generally been that smaller boards are more effective because they can hold more candid discussions and make quicker decisions and because they are less easily controlled by management than is a large, unwieldy group of directors. With respect to board independence, the variable of greatest interest in the empirical literature has been the proportion of outside directors on the board. The hypothesis is that directors who are members of the firm's management or who are affiliated with those managers (generally termed inside directors and affiliated/grey directors, respectively) are less effective as monitors of management than are those directors who have no family or business ties with the firm's management (so-called outside directors).[1]

1. RELATED RESEARCH

Given the many different ways in which a company can structure its board of directors, the question arises what board characteristics are really most effective in providing good corporate governance. Below, we review empirical findings from the corporate-

---

1 Independent directors, by definition, have no tie to the company other than through their role as a board of director member. Grey directors represent outside directors who have some non-board affiliation with the firm. Non-board affiliations with the company results from the outside director being a relative of management, or a former employee, current supplier, customer, consultant, or outside legal counsel for the company.

governance literature on the impact that board characteristics have in five fields: corporate performance, corporate decisions, stock prices, financial-statement fraud and earnings manipulation.

a. BOARD CHARACTERISTICS AND CORPORATE PERFORMANCE

Especially the impact of three board characteristics on corporate performance has been investigated: board size, board independence, and separation of Chairman and CEO positions.

Board size and corporate performance

With respect to size, the hypothesis tested has generally been that smaller boards are more effective for the reasons mentioned above (candid discussions, quick decisions, less easily controlled by management). Jensen (1993) points out that when boards get beyond seven or eight people, they are less likely to function effectively and are easier for the CEO to control: when boards get to be too big, agency problems[2] increase and the board becomes more symbolic and less a part of the management process. In contrast, others believe larger boards may be more valuable because of the greater diversity of knowledge and experience available.

Empirically, there is substantial but non-unanimous evidence that board size and corporate performance tend to be negatively related. Yermack (1996) states that the only evidence (at the time) there is that board size is negatively correlated with corporate performance. He adds that companies with small boards also exhibit more favourable financial ratios and provide stronger CEO incentives. Similarly, Eisenberg *et al.* (1998) report a negative correlation between performance and board size for small and midsize Finnish firms. Bhagat and Black (2000), however, find much weaker evidence of a correlation between board size and corporate performance. One study documents a beneficial effect for size: Chaganti *et al.* (1985) find that firms filing for Chapter 11 bankruptcy protection have smaller boards than firms that avoid distress, suggesting that a larger board may be more effective in preventing corporate failure.

---

2 There is an agency contract between the stakeholders – the principals in the relationship – and the managers who, being their agents, are supposed to act in the principals' best interests. The underlying concern is that, when stakeholders are imperfectly informed about the managers' available options and the degree of diligence and effort they put into their jobs, then the managers may seek their own interests at the expense of the principals. This concern leads to efforts to reduce the information asymmetry and, by the same token, also the agency problems. For example, the board acts as the "eyes" of the shareholders, who pay the board members for their work.

Board independence and corporate performance

Board independence is generally measured by the proportion of outside directors on the board. The hypothesis is that directors that are also members of the company's management or who are affiliated with those managers are less effective as monitors of management than are directors that have no family or business ties to firm management. Fama and Jensen (1983) emphasize that independent directors have incentives to build reputations as expert monitors. One has to realize however that, to a director, a reputation as one who does not make trouble for CEOs is potentially valuable as well.

The above does not mean that all members should be outsiders: a reasonable number of inside directors on the board can add value too. If a board contains a mix of inside, independent, and perhaps also affiliated directors, a whole range of skills and knowledge is brought in. Inside directors can add value because they are well informed about the firm, whereas independent directors are relatively ignorant about the company. Perhaps independent directors will act more quickly than inside directors if something goes wrong; but they may do the wrong thing if their deliberations are not leavened by the information available to inside directors (Bhagat and Black, 2001). In the same vein, Bhagat and Black (1999) find it not *a priori* obvious that independence without knowledge or incentives leads to better director performance than knowledge and strong incentives without independence. They argue that it may be better to build a board with some knowledgeable, incentivized inside directors and some independent directors, who might thereby become better informed and could also be better incentivized than many independent directors are today.

Another perspective on board independence is provided by Hermalin and Weisbach (1998). They argue that a board's independence is the result of a bargaining game between the board and the CEO. The CEO prefers a less independent board while the board prefers to maintain its independence. When the CEO has bargaining power, specifically when the CEO has demonstrated high skills by performing exceptionally well, the board's independence declines. Conversely, poor corporate performance reduces a CEO's perceived ability relative to that of a potential replacement, increasing the likelihood that the board will replace him.

Empirical research generally concludes that board independence is not significantly related to corporate performance. Denis (2001) and Hermalin and Weisbach (2003) state that in most studies there is no significant relation between corporate performance and the proportion of outsiders. There are several possible reasons for the non-significant relation between corporate performance and the proportion of outsiders. First, outsiders may typically have been brought in *following* poor performance. Evidence by Bhagat and Black (2000) confirms that low-profitability firms respond by increasing board independence. But they state that this strategy does not work: most of these firms do not achieve the sought-after improved profitability. Because of this effect, it then looks as if outside directors are associated with poor corporate performance. A second explanation may be errors in variables: plenty of directors classified as outside may be not genuine outsiders, as the data overlook connections with management. Another possible explanation is that boards are perhaps effective only in extreme situations, like fraud, and not so much in steering day-to-day performance.

But a non-trivial minority of researchers (Yermack 1996; Agrawal and Knoeber 1996; Klein 1998) finds that firms with a high percentage of independent directors actually perform worse. Finally, Klein (1998) argues that independent directors can add value indeed – but only if they are embedded in the right committee structure. She finds positive associations between corporate performance and the percentage of insiders on the board's finance and investment committees. The market also explicitly acknowledges this by rewarding firms whose boards significantly increase their percentage of insiders on either committee.

Separation of Chairman and CEO positions: impact on corporate performance

Most Best Practice Codes on corporate governance recommend, among other things, that boards include a number of outside directors and that the positions of chair and CEO be held by different individuals[3]. Jensen (1993) points out that when the CEO also holds the position of the chairman of the board, internal control systems fail, as the board cannot effectively perform its key functions including those of evaluating and firing CEOs. Similarly, Fama and Jensen (1983) argue that concentration of decision management and decision control in one individual reduces a board's effectiveness in monitoring top management.

In contrast, Brickley *et al.* (1997) point out that separate CEO and chairman positions may engender costs in monitoring the chairman, information sharing costs between the CEO and the chairman, and incentive costs associated with a succession process in which CEOs are promised the chairman title. These costs may offset the monitoring advantages that arise from a separate CEO-chairman leadership structure. In practice, U.S. firms tend to combine the two positions in one and the same person. Rechner and Dalton (1991) find, in their sample of 141 firms, that only 21.3% separate the titles. Similarly, Pi and Timme (1993) find a separation of titles in approximately 25% of the banks they study.

Empirically, there is more evidence that firms perform better when the CEO and chairman functions are separated; true, some studies find no clear effect, but no study documents a reverse link. The separatists include Pi and Timme (1993), Baliga *et al.*

[3] This is for example the case in the Belgian Lippens Code (2004); but even longer ago the UK Cadbury Code (1992) included such recommendations (note that the latter code has been replaced by the Combined Code on Corporate Govnerance in 2003).

(1996), and Rechner and Dalton (1991), who all find that firms combining the CEO-chairman titles perform worse than firms that do not combine them. In the same vein, Goyal and Park (2000) point out that the sensitivity of top executive turnover to corporate performance is significantly lower for firms that vest the titles of CEO and chairman in the same individual. But others, notably Brickley *et al.* (1997), and Vafeas & Theodorou (1998), find no convincing evidence either way.

This finishes our discussion of the impact of the board's characteristics on corporate performance. We now turn to their impact on some key corporate decisions.

b. BOARD CHARACTERISTICS AND CORPORATE DECISIONS

In the corporate governance literature the emphasis is on three groups of corporate decisions on which board characteristics have a significant impact: the decision to dismiss a poorly performing CEO, decisions about CEO compensation and decisions about takeover bids and acquisitions.

Dismissal of poorly performing CEOs

A key part of the monitoring process is the replacement of the CEO when circumstances warrant such a decision. Rather than making day-to-day decisions, boards appear to play a crucial role in picking the firm's CEO, and view their primary responsibility as monitoring and potentially replacing him (Hermalin and Weisbach, 2001). An active, not management-beholden board will presumably make the necessary change sooner – a good thing, as a poorly performing management team creates more harm to the overall enterprise the longer it is in place. It would then follow that companies where the CEO is replaced expeditiously in times of poor performance have more active and effective monitoring boards than those companies where an ineffective CEO remains in office for longer periods of time.

The empirical evidence on this issue is, again, not quite conclusive. Most, but not all, studies conclude that smaller and/or independent boards are more effective overseers of the CEO than larger boards. Weisbach (1988), for instance, finds that poorly performing CEOs are more rapidly dismissed in companies with a smaller board and/or a greater proportion of outside directors. Yermack (1996) provides similar results for the relation between board size and CEO dismissal, while Perry (2000) confirms that the likelihood of CEO dismissal in the case of poor corporate performance is positively associated with board independence. Perry further adds that this likelihood also rises when outside directors are at least partly compensated with stock-option plans. (Thus, in this instance, providing directors with a financial stake does seem to help in aligning the interests of directors with those of shareholders.)

For Belgium, Renneboog (2000) finds that the percentage of number of outside directors is positively associated with the dismissal of top management. Finally, Goyal and Park (2000) find that the sensitivity of top executive turnover to the firm's performance is significantly lower for firms that vest the titles of CEO and chairman in the same individual. These results are consistent with the view that, in firms where CEO en chairman are united in one person, the lack of independent leadership makes it difficult for the board to remove poorly performing managers.

Some studies are agnostic. For instance, Kang and Shivdasani (1995) are unable to document a definite relation between the presence of outside directors and the sensitivity of CEO turnover to performance for Japanese firms. One study flatly disagrees with mainstream thinking. Franks, Mayer and Renneboog (2001), notably, examine a sample of poorly-performing firms in the UK and find that boards dominated by outside directors actually impede discipline of poorly performing managers.

CEO compensation

The separation of ownership and control in large modern corporations gives rise to an agency problem. A firm's owners delegate many of the control and decision rights to a group of managers who often hold insignificant ownership positions. The owners often hope to alleviate the agency problem by designing managerial incentive contracts that better align the incentives of managers with the firm's shareholders, like having management hold common stock of the firm or stock options.

Whether this works or not is reviewed in Section c, below. The issue discussed here is which boards go farthest, that is, what board characteristics affect the degree of sensitivity of executive pay to performance (Dennis and McConnell, 2003). Overall, the empirical results are conclusive: smaller boards and/or a greater proportion of outside directors are associated with more sensitive CEO compensation plans. Core *et al.* (1999) find that firms with weaker governance structures tend to pay their CEOs more. In particular, they find that CEO pay rises with the number of outsiders appointed by the CEO, the number of directors over age 69, board size, and the number of directors holding additional directorships. In addition, Core *et al.* (1999) find that CEO pay increases when a board contains interlocking directors (i.e. each director sits on the other's board, reducing the independence of both), who are more likely to be influenced by the CEO.

Hermalin and Weisbach (1998) find that in companies with a smaller board and/or a greater proportion of outside directors, CEO compensation plans are more sensitive to CEO performance. Likewise, Milliron (2000) finds that CEO incentive pay is positively associated with both the degree of director independence and the degree of director accountability (measured by directors' stock ownership). Finally, research results by Yermack (1996) show that the pay-performance relation for CEOs decreases with board size, suggesting that small boards give CEOs larger incentives and force them to bear more risk than do large boards.

Takeover bids and acquisitions

Byrd and Hickman (1992) point out that the board of directors is virtually certain to be involved in any takeover attempt because acquisitions are major investments that may alter the strategic direction of the firm and thus affect the wealth of the shareholders. Outside directors can play a very important role in monitoring the acquisition. They may be involved in other firms that have done acquisitions and therefore be more objective in evaluating the potential benefits and costs of an acquisition. They may also have special information about the target firm's industry or the target firm itself. Byrd and Hickman (1992) argue that the objectivity of outside directors is particularly important in monitoring the acquisition process when managers' empire-building ambitions or executive pride conflict with shareholders' interests. Hirshleifer and Thakor (1994) point out that, even with a well-functioning takeover market, the wealth of the firm's shareholders still depends on the board, which determines whether to bid or not and how much is being offered. Brickley *et al.* (1994) argue that a higher percentage of outside directors is beneficial to the quality of the board's decisions regarding acquisitions and poison pills.[4]

The empirical evidence is, again, mixed. Byrd and Hickman (1992) find evidence of a non-linear relationship between the fraction of independent directors on the acquiror's board and the shareholder- wealth effects of tender-offer bids, expressed as higher announcement-date abnormal returns. Specifically, while this relationship is positive over most of its range, it turns negative when the fraction of independent directors is extremely high (over 60%). This suggests that it is possible to have too many independent outside directors. They further report that tender-offer bidders with predominantly independent boards earn roughly zero stock-price returns on average, while bidders without such boards suffer statistically significant losses of 1.8% on average. This finding indicates that the market perceives firms with independent boards as making better – *i.e.* less bad – acquisitions. However, Subrahmanyam *et al.* (1997) observe the opposite tendency for bank acquisitions: a high proportion of outside directors predicts lower stock-price returns for the acquiring bank. One study, finally, looks at the effect of the acquiree's board. Cotter *et al.* (1997) find that when the target's board contains a majority of outside directors, the target receives about a 20 percent higher return than a similar firm without a majority of outside directors

4 In the case of poison pills, the incumbent management of a corporation attempts to discourage a hostile takeover by increasing the takeover cost, *e.g.* by issuing new preferred shares carrying onerous redemption rights in the event of new corporate ownership or by issuing new voting stock, at a low price, to friendly shareholders.

on their board. This finding suggests that, at least at the acquiree's side, outside directors do a better job of negotiating on behalf of shareholders during tender offers than do insiders.

We now turn to a third avenue via which the board's characteristics may matter: shareholder value.

c. BOARD CHARACTERISTICS AND STOCK PRICES

In the empirical research on the impact of board characteristics on stock prices there are basically two angles: First, can one detect any association between the presence of certain board characteristics and the stock price evolution? Second, is there a detectable stock-market reaction to some of the changes in board characteristics?

Impact of board characteristics on stock price evolution

Hambrick and Jackson (2000) find that superior shareholder returns are positively associated with the degree of ownership by outside directors, and that three to five percent of their personal net worth tends to be enough to serve as an effective incentive. As a consequence the authors propose the installation of a stock-purchase-matching fund that would match the director's own investments into company stock. Recall also the study by Cotter *et al.* (1997): in a takeover the target shareholder receives about a 20 percent higher return than a similar firm without a majority of outside directors on their board. Thus, both studies associate outsider majorities with higher returns.

Stock market's reaction to changes in board characteristics

When board characteristics change, the market's reaction depends on how the market view this change to affect firm's effectiveness. A positive market reaction, notably, is associated with an expected improvement of the firm's effectiveness and *vice versa.* Rosenstein and Wyatt (1990) examine the impact of the appointment of outside versus inside directors. They find that the appointment of a new outside member of the board of directors has a positive effect on the stock price of the firm, whereas the appointment of a new inside member of the board of directors has no clear effect. Bhagat and Black (2001) argue that these findings could reflect signalling effects: appointing an additional outside director could signal that a company plans to address its business problems, even if board composition does not affect the company's ability to address these problems.

In addition, Shivdansani and Yermack (1999) observe that stock price reactions to independent-director appointments are significantly lower when the CEO is involved in the selection. Borokhovich *et al.* (1996) notice that the outside directors have a preference for appointing outside CEOs. The stock market reaction to an outside appointment is also favourable.

Broadening the issue, Rodriguez and Anson (2001) examine the market reaction to announcements by Spanish firms that they will comply with the Spanish Code of Best Practice, which contains 23 recommendations that aim to strengthen the supervisory role of the board of directors. They report that the stock prices react positively to announcements of compliance when such announcements imply a major restructuring of the board; this reaction is also stronger for firms that have been performing poorly.

The fourth area where the board's characteristics may matter is earnings management.

d. BOARD CHARACTERISTICS AND EARNINGS MANAGEMENT

For most firms, management compensation is explicitly or implicitly a function of some earnings-based performance measure. The emphasis on earnings encourages managers to meet earnings targets. Schipper (1989) defines earnings management as a purposeful intervention in the external financial reporting process, with a view to obtaining a private gain for stockholders or managers. Stockholders will gain when earnings management is used to signal managers' private information (Healy and Palepu, 1995). However, stockholders may lose when earnings management results in abnormal private gains to managers. Such gains could take the form of increased compensation (Healy, 1985) or reduced likelihood of dismissal when true performance is low (Weisbach, 1988).

The actual existence of earnings management itself is well established. Degeorge *et al.* (1999) find that managers appear to systematically manipulate reported earnings downwards when pre-managed earnings exceed threshold earnings by a substantial amount. Similarly, Healy (1985), Gaver *et al.* (1995) and Holthausen *et al.* (1995) report evidence of income-decreasing accounting choices when managers' accounting-based bonuses are already at their maximum. The explanation that first comes to mind is that managers prefer to shift abnormal positive earnings forward in order to make future thresholds easier to attain. But another possible explanation is that managers are reluctant to report large gains because of fears that their performance target will be ratcheted up in the future.

The board can play an important role in monitoring management activity and financial reporting. Peasnell *et al.* (2000) argue that the board's effectiveness in monitoring the financial reports will depend on the ability of outside directors to understand earnings management methods. There are at least two reasons for having confidence in outside directors' general ability in this respect. First, outside directors often have a financial background. Second, outside directors frequently hold senior management positions in other large corporations (Fama and Jensen, 1983). As such, they are likely to be familiar with financial reporting from a senior-management perspective. We again review the empirical impact of board size and degree of independence on the board's effectiveness in restraining earnings management.

Board independence and earnings management

An effective board is a board that constrains earnings management and financial reporting manipulation. Peasnell *et al.* (2000) find that firms with a higher proportion of outside board members are associated with less income-increasing earnings management when pre-managed earnings fall below either zero or last year's reported earnings. These results suggest that such earnings management is motivated by an attempt to delay reporting bad news, rather than to signal future performance. Peasnell *et al.* conclude that outside directors appear to play an important monitoring role in terms of helping to uphold the integrity and credibility of published financial statements. But the authors find little evidence that outside directors constrain downward manipulations when pre-managed earnings are very high. These results suggest that financial statement monitoring by outsiders is asymmetric, with the main focus on constraining income-increasing manipulations.

Similarly, Agrawal and Chadha (2003) find less income-increasing earnings management in firms whose outside board members have experience as board member with the firm and with other firms. They also find that income-decreasing earnings management is less pronounced the larger the board, the higher the ownership stakes in the firm held by non-executive directors, and the more experience board members have.

Board size and earnings management

For Hong Kong, Ching *et al.* (2002) examine whether the incidence of earnings management around Seasoned Equity Offerings (SEOs) depends on corporate-governance structures. SEO firms that have larger board size turn out to indulge in more earnings management around SEOs. This result is consistent with Jensen's (1993) view that smaller boards provide more of a controlling function than do larger boards. In contrast to expectations, Van der Bauwhede *et al.* (2000) find for Belgium that the extent of earnings management is lower when the size of the board is smaller or larger than the optimal size.

We now turn to the fifth and last field potentially affected by board composition and size: the quality of the financial statements, and especially the absence or presence of fraud.

e. BOARD CHARACTERISTICS AND FINANCIAL STATEMENT QUALITY / FRAUD

As was pointed out in the intro, boards of directors are widely held to play an important role monitoring top management. Outside board members are assumed to be better at alleviating agency conflicts between shareholders and top management. A possible conflict arises when managers maximize their own utility at the expense of the shareholder through opportunistic financial statements or even outright fraud.

Dechow *et al.* (1996) report that firms with a majority of inside directors and without an audit committee are more likely to commit financial fraud, compared to a control sample matched by industry and size. Similarly, Beasley (1996) finds that firms that commit fraud have fewer independent directors than matched control firms that did not commit fraud. One should not necessarily conclude that the inclusion of outside members on the board of directors could increase the board's effectiveness at monitoring management for the prevention of financial statement fraud. It is, indeed, also possible that managers that are more prone to commit fraud also fight harder against the inclusion of independent board members, so that manager fraud propensity drives both the likelihood of fraud and the degree of board independence.

Abbott *et al.* (2002) find that the likelihood of financial misstatement fraud is higher for firms with larger boards or whose CEO also doubles as chair. However, unlike Beasley (1996) they find no significant relationship between the degree of independence and financial-statement fraud.

This finishes our review of the literature. We now turn to the actual situation in Belgium and then to the related debate in the Table Round sessions.

2. ACTUAL PRACTICE IN BELGIUM

We look at the situation in 48 quoted Belgian companies whose disclosure behavior is studied in Chapter 6. These 48 are, basically, the entire surviving Euronext-Brussels list of non-financials, apart from a few cases with missing data. We looked at the annual reports for 2001 and 2003 and recorded the characteristics relevant for the present survey.

Table 1: Boards of directors: general characteristics

		Avge	Med	High	Low
Number of board members (BM)	2003	9.3	9	16	4
	2001	9.4	9	19	4
Share of non-executives	2003	65.0%	66.6%	100%	12.5%
	2001	74.7%	77.8%	100%	42.9%
Share of independents	2003	39.5%	40.0%	91.7%	0%
	2001	39.3%	37.5%	87.5%	0%
Number of board meetings/yr	2003	7.3	6	21	3
	2001	7	6	17	3
Number of ExecCom members (if any)		6.7	6	17	3

Table 1 presents some general descriptive data regarding the board of directors. A typical board consists of nine members, with basically no change over the two-year interval. The relative share of non-executives is systematically and substantially above one-half, but there seems to be a pronounced fall, from three out of four in 2001 to two out of three in 2003 – not a change in the direction that is conventionally viewed as desirable. The share of independents members is below one-half, but is not trending downwards. A typical board meets 6 to 7 times a year, with some right-skewness, that is, outliers at the up-side.

Table 2 tells us that in 65-70 percent of the boards the CEO does not chair the board; so in this respect we are more similar to the UK situation than the U.S. situation (where the personal union occurs in about 70 percent of the boards). There is no sign of any upward trend; to the contrary, perhaps, but the period is short and the number of observations small. There is a growing openness regarding total compensation for the board or committee, but far less so for individuals, especially when it comes top executives. Note that, by now, all this information has become mandatory.

Table 2: Further descriptives on Board and Executive Committee

	2003	2001
No split between Chairman / CEO roles	35.4%	29.3%
Publishes most important rules for the BoD	89.6%	92.7%
Publishes individual compensation of Board members	18.7%	2.4%
Publishes total compensation for the ExCom	66.7%	46.3%
Publishes individual compensation of ExCom	0%	0%

Purely fixed compensation, in the Board of Directors, occurs in half of the cases (56 percent if one includes zero compensations). Thus, 44 percent receive at least part of their compensation in contingent form, and one (out of 34 companies that provide information) even has no fixed component at all. In the executive committee, variable compensations (and even purely variable compensations) are markedly more frequent than in the board, but the typical audit committee sensibly prefers to work with just fixed (or zero) compensation.

Table 3: Compensation in the Board, Executive Committee, or Audit Committee, 2003

	Board	ExCom	AudCom
All members receive a fixed compensation	50.00%	20%	70%
All members receive a mixture (fixed + variable)	29.40%	64%	5%
Compensation differs executives *v.* non-exec	11.80%	–	–
Members receive no compensation	5.90%	–	25%
There is no fixed component in the compensation	2.90%	16%	–

Virtually all boards work with committees; remuneration, audit and executive committees are quite prevalent; the number of nomination committees may be catching up, though.

Table 4. Prevalence of committees within the Board

	2003	2001
Remuneration Committee	77.1%	85.4%
Audit Committee	77.1%	75.6%
Executive Committee	75.0%	73.2%
Nomination Committee	41.6%	34.1%

3. ROUND-TABLE DISCUSSION

In this section we report on the discussions that took place amongst the participants of five the round table sessions. We also provide the results of the questionnaires that were filled out by those participants about certain potential or popular best practice governance rules (see, also chapter 1 for more background information).

Board organisation: two models

There are generally two visions related to the board organisation, as one capital provider points out: the "Rijnland" model where the board represents the various stakeholders and the Anglo-Saxon model where the board is generally composed of just representatives of shareholders. The latter model comprises two variants: the American and the British version. In the U.S., the board is to a large extent composed of "friends" of the CEO, who also typically chairs the board, whereas the modal UK board achieves more of a balance between executives and non-executives.

Board composition has an impact on the decisions taken in the board and its general functioning. However, the outcome of both Anglo- Saxon and the "Rijnland" models should be comparable if the board takes a long-term vision – because in a long-term perspective, the other stakeholders' interests must necessarily be considered even in a shareholder-focused board. And the long-run view is what the board should be about: it should make sure that the firm evolves in the desired direction, that it creates value on a long-term basis, rather than steering day-to-day performance. Enron was an extreme example of a short-term perspective.

Board organisation and corporate governance

A representative of the capital providers states that the structuring of responsibilities and the composition of the board are important for two reasons. The first is that it affects the supply of information to the members of the board. The U.S. model faces a problem concerning this supply because the CEO controls the internal information and the members have fewer outside links, whereas the British model has the advantage that the information supply is diverse, not so much determined by the CEO as in the U.S. The second reason why the composition of the board matters is that it affects the degree of effectiveness of the trust relation/cooperation between the executives and the non-executives. Both parties should respect each other's responsibilities of and strike a balance between cooperation and control. The most difficult task of the board is to give sufficient support to the CEO and at the same time maintain a sufficient level of control. Thus, this spokesman from the capital markets concludes, the debate about corporate governance is concentrated around two main issues: information supply and the trust relation.

An executive adds that one danger with the U.S. trust model (or lack-of-trust model) is that members of a firm get obsessed with obtaining legal coverage. This is the negation of trust. The essence of corporate governance is that the firm takes optimal strategic decisions to create value. Corporate governance is not a goal in itself: it is a means to achieve fundamental value creation. This requires trust and cooperation, not legal hedging games.

An auditor notices a similarity with an long-standing issue in accounting: lawyers and accountants seem to differ about whether corporate governance should become more rules-based or more principles-based. The international view among accountants tends to be that accounting should become more principles-based and governance more rules-based, while lawyers tend to favour it the other way around. This is part of an ages-old substance-versus-form debate. However, while rules can always be made and lofty principles can always be proclaimed, what is important is what people are really doing.

All by all, the parties agree that many corporate scandals can be explained by the short-term perspective adopted by the board and executive committee. But also the market's perspective has shortened as the demand for more recent information and the sensitivity of the share-price reaction to it have increased substantially. Thus, the whole system becomes myopic, leading to various scandals. But the financing structure of the firm should be considered too, an executive points out. In a German model where banks are also shareholders and represent other shareholders, the short-term perspective is less of a problem.

Board size

Table 5: Board size

"No ideal size can be defined, but in general Boards should be kept small in size (with a maximum of 10 to 14 members)."				
	Agree	Disagree	Depends	Blank
Board of directors	7/7	0/7	0/7	0/7
Executive Committee	14/14	0/14	0/14	0/14
Capital providers	9/9	0/9	0/9	0/9
External auditors	11/11	0/11	0/11	0/11
Academics	8/8	0/8	0/8	0/8

As is shown in Table 5, all parties agree that board size should be kept small. Board members and executives argue that a minimum size is needed to obtain a good mix of competences (financial expertise, sectoral savvy and strategic knowledge). It is important to have a certain diversity in the way of thinking and doing in order to have a multiple perspective. On the other hand, the more members there are, the more laborious the meetings become; just think of finding a meeting date where most can be present. In addition, a small board increases the members' feeling of involvement and relevance and makes it easier to establish good and frequent contacts with the executive committee, which helps to get to know the firm.

Still, all parties agree that the quality of the board is definitely more important than board size, which often depends on the past. The focus should be on the quality of board members rather than their number. For instance, board members should have a notion of what is happening in a firm and its industry, and they should at least be able to understand a balance sheet. An auditor points out that the CEO also more easily manipulates a board where too many members are public figures, chosen merely to add prestige to the board.

Board composition

There is a general agreement that there should be sufficient diversity concerning age and perspectives. It is furthermore important to create a balance between the different parties in the board. The board is expected to act as one body, and a mixed board composition contributes to joint responsibility taking. However, a clear definition of the different roles in the board and the common responsibilities is also crucial. Also information and trust are very important issues for a well-functioning board. Therefore, mixed composition is beneficial as it enhances the quality of information available to board members. But new board members should also share the culture of the firm. Diversity is important, but so is a shared culture.

Before any selection process is initiated, the current composition should be evaluated on its strengths and weaknesses and a profile of an ideal new member should be specified. Choosing the correct person is difficult, and the process gets easier the better the qualities of a candidate are known.

The CEO as a board member?

One of the executives on the Round-Table meeting states, to much agreement, that it is not recommendable to have people of the executive committee in the board other than the CEO, because the board should be able to take its decisions independently from the executives. And if other executives are allowed to be present at all, they should not participate as a member. Capital providers agree, and add that whenever the role and the functioning of CEO is being discussed, there should be a separate meeting with only independent directors, because it is necessary to have an open discussion.

Board independence

Table 6: Inside/outside ratio on the board of directors

"The ratio outside/inside directors on the BOD should exceed unity, because this would have a positive impact on corporate performance."				
	Agree	Disagree	Depends	Blank
Board of directors	5/7	0/7	1/7	1/7
Executive Committee	6/14	6/14	1/14	1/14
Capital providers	9/9	0/9	0/9	0/9
External auditors	5/11	6/11	0/11	0/11
Academics	2/8	4/8	0/8	2/8

The majority of our round table participants, with the notable exceptions of executives and auditors, agree that there is a need for board members with a strong backbone, so to speak, who are not influenced by a high remuneration or the visibility associated with sitting on the board of a prestigious firm. The board needs people who can stand up to management if things go wrong.

Independence is much more a practical than a formal issue, many of the round table members stress. What is important is the action the board member undertakes to defend the interests of the firm. Also the "inside" board members should share the notion of honesty and independence. Auditors agree: independence is more a state of mind. There are a number of formal criteria that may provide indications *re* the degree of independence, but these offer no guarantee for genuine independence. Rather than looking for neat definitions of independence and agonizing whether a particular contractual relationship harms independence, it may be more important to require full disclosure of any such contractual relationships that may or may not weaken the independence of board members.

There was some debate as to what objectives are primarily served by independence. One board member posits that the only reason why independence is important is that there should be sufficient countervailing power: to avoid that the firm be managed in the interest of the management or a subset of shareholders – *e.g.* the reference shareholder – or the employees rather than the shareholders as a group or the body of all stakeholders. Auditors agree that independent directors are there in the first place to add value by providing independent advice and help in taking the best decisions; but directors' independence should also serve good governance by making sure that financial statements give a true and fair view.

Table 7: Role of outside directors

"Outside directors play an important monitoring role in terms of helping to uphold the integrity and credibility of published financial statements."				
	Agree	Disagree	Depends	Blank
Board of directors	6/7	0/7	0/7	1/7
Executive Committee	14/14	0/14	0/14	0/14
Capital providers	8/9	0/9	1/9	0/9
External auditors	11/11	0/11	0/11	0/11
Academics	8/8	0/8	0/8	0/8

Should the CEO also chair the board?

By and large, executives agree that the CEO and chair should be separated, but the more fundamental issue remains the power of the board to go against the CEO. Two examples illustrate the importance of the separation: acquisitions and the case of an underperforming CEO. When acquisition proposals reach the board, executives are generally much more enthusiastic than board members, who often are divided on the issue. The separation of the functions of CEO and chair of the board should then permit all voices to be heard before any decision is taken. In the case of a poorly performing CEO, it is easier to take action if there is a strong person, like the chairman, who can take the initiative. In general, the board members in our panel see the relation between the chair and CEO as complementary. The chair is expected to stimulate the CEO to provide timely, relevant information, and by doing so to alert the board of any possible problem way before the situation gets out of hand. They add that there should also be a good interaction between CEO and the chairs of the different committees within the board, to build up interpersonal relations and strengthen the mutual commitment to improve corporate performance.

However, some executives take an it-all-depends view. For instance, the presence of reference shareholders in the board may weaken the need for separation of the two functions because such a presence already favors the diversion of opinions and balance of power. Likewise, if much is being delegated from the board to the executive committee, then a personal union of the functions of CEO and chair facilitates the (co)operation of the two layers of decision-making.

Should board members receive stock-based compensation?

Table 8: Stock-based compensation?

"Board members should receive stock-based compensation."				
	Agree	**Disagree**	**Depends**	**Blank**
Board of directors	0/7	4/7	3/7	0/7
Executive Committee	5/14	8/14	0/14	1/14
Capital providers	3/9	5/9	1/9	0/9
External auditors	1/11	9/11	1/11	0/11
Academics	5/8	2/8	1/8	0/8

The common opinion is that it is acceptable, but not necessary, that board members receive stock-based compensation. A capital provider argues that stock-based compensation for board members is a good way to align the interests of board member and shareholders; directors will take their jobs seriously and will make sure that the board functions effectively.

This sparked off a lively debate regarding the merits of stock-option plans relative to straight stock holdings. All parties agree that a long-term perspective is crucial in a stock-option plan. Stock options are very dangerous if they are used in a short-term perspective, as too much stress is put on short-term results. Incentives should be given so that value is created in long run. An academic argues that the problems of short-term share-price manipulation and boosting of share-price volatility can be resolved by working with Asian-tail options, which work with average prices over longer term (*e.g.* three years) instead of the price of one single day. This eliminates the incentive for short-term earnings manipulation. Another important requirement for stock option compensation, a capital provider emphasizes, is that the total value of these options should not be excessive relative to the net assets of the director, otherwise the incentives to manipulate become too strong.

However, not everyone is even convinced that options do work as an incentive scheme. A capital provider points out that stock options are for 99% influenced by the general market's level and volatility and other factors unrelated to the performance of an individual within the firm. In addition, exercising the options dilutes the other shares, thus leading to a situation where directors win and shareholders lose. Things are better, our financier continues, if the board members hold stock of the firm, bought at the normal market price: there is no redistribution of wealth, and the incentives to work hard then generate a win-win outcome. An additional drawback, an auditor points out, is that stock-option compensation creates problems with the financial statements: should the EOP be expensed at all, and if so, how? Another states that from the point of view of appearance of independence towards all the stakeholders, it is simply better that board members have no stock options. Board members share his concern and add that there should be an efficient overseeing mechanism to prevent abuse. Lastly, one executive remarks, when stock options are awarded, board liability can be a problem because in the first six months after the options have been granted the board cannot take important decisions. This may be one more reason why stock options are rarely awarded to the board.

Should the board clearly define performance measures for the CEO?

There is near-perfect unanimity that performance targets should be set for the CEO, as is apparent from Table 9.

Table 9: Performance targets for the CEO

"Clear performance measures should be defined by the board to evaluate the CEO's performance."				
	Agree	Disagree	Depends	Blank
Board of directors	6/7	0/7	1/7	0/7
Executive Committee	13/14	1/14	0/14	0/14
Capital providers	9/9	0/9	0/9	0/9
External auditors	11/11	0/11	0/11	0/11
Academics	7/8	1/8	0/8	0/8

One of the auditors opens the debate with the assertion that the performance measurements should logically fit in with the board's strategy for the company. That is, these benchmarks should be determined consistently with the strategic plan of the company. A board member agrees, and amplifies that general objectives should be set, rather than just specific numbers. The board can indicate the direction in which the company should evolve, and whether this means a 14% or a 15% growth rate is less important. Furthermore, the criteria should cover not just financial matters, but also strategic issues; and a time perspective should be included too. An auditor adds that negotiation between the CEO and the board is required. (This, executives interject, should certainly be the case; also the compensation committee should be involved.) But there is a risk here: the CEO will most likely want a broad set of vaguish performance measures instead of a single figure. But in the end of the negotiation, there should still be one key standard, or a few key standards, that really can be measured, otherwise the whole thing becomes pointless. Notably, if the board allows too much broadening of the performance measures and too qualitative a set of standards, there is a danger of ending up with only the appearance of performance measurement. This also may weaken the board's ability to dismiss a really poorly performing CEO. Executives, lastly, point out that stock-price related criteria should not be used to evaluate CEO performance, as the CEO does not control the stock-market environment.

Should a poorly performing CEO be dismissed by the Board?

With very few exceptions, in Table 10 the various parties agree that a poorly performing CEO should be dismissed by the board. Executives hasten to add that any such decision should be taken with great caution. The board should first verify the presence of an acceptable replacement. In addition, the firm's situation and the structure of the balance sheet should be taken into consideration: some CEOs may perform excellently in crisis situation, but may stop functioning well when the firm become stable or enters a growth period (or *vice versa*). Another executive posits that a deteriorating balance sheet structure is one of the clearest triggers to dismiss a CEO. A third one replies that the balance sheet is also the responsibility of the board and that, when the balance sheet is obviously in a bad condition already, the dismissal of the CEO comes too late, in fact.

Table 10: Dismissal of the CEO

"Poorly performing CEO's should be dismissed by the BOD."				
	Agree	Disagree	Depends	Blank
Board of directors	7/7	0/7	0/7	0/7
Executive Committee	14/14	0/14	0/14	0/14
Capital providers	8/9	1/9	0/9	0/9
External auditors	10/11	0/11	0/11	1/11
Academics	7/8	1/8	0/8	0/8

Controversially, one capital provider asserts that a board should never take the decision to dismiss the CEO, because this may result in internal struggles in the board. Instead, the general assembly of shareholders should rule on the CEO's dismissal. Other capital providers do not agree and reply that, in this set-up, the board may feel it is no longer accountable for performance: the situation cannot be remedied when crucial decisions are in the hands of the General Assembly.

How to end the CEO's term in less distressed circumstances? Executives suggest that CEOs can only operate effectively in a firm for ten or twelve years, as the CEO might get too cosily imbedded in the firm and hence lose perspective. In addition, if a strong CEO stays on too long, talented people in the firm lose career perspectives and motivation and hence vote with their feet.

Do outsiders depend on information supply by the insiders?

There is a consensus among all parties that non-executives do depend on executives for internal information (Table 11). Committees play an important role here, one of the executive discussants notes. Information and recommendations from the committees are used in the decision process of the board. Once the committee has discussed the technical issues, the board may then initiate a more general debate.

Table 11: Non-executives depend on executives' information

"Non-executives depend on executives for internal information."				
	Agree	Disagree	Depends	Blank
Board of directors	7/7	0/7	0/7	0/7
Executive Committee	12/14	1/14	0/14	1/14
Capital providers	8/9	1/9	0/9	0/9
External auditors	10/11	1/11	0/11	0/11
Academics	6/8	2/8	0/8	0/8

Another discussant remarks that the figures and other data presented to the board and the committees are in both cases provided by the executives. The executives may have coloured these figures, even when all accounting rules are abided by. It is therefore very important for the board and committee members to agree upon certain formal accounting rules and underlying accounting principles. It is furthermore important that the board receive summarized information, and that access to information be equal for all board members.

One executive recommends that all information that is provided to the committee members also be provided to all general board members. However, this opinion is not shared by all board members and executives. These reply that if all the details are again presented in the board, there will be too much duplication of work. The board should be informed about the key numbers and facts and also get access to detailed information of the committees if desired. There is however a difference between a right of access to detailed information and redoing the work of the committees in the board.

Should the number of boards one individual can sit on be capped – at, say, 5?

Table 12: Limits to the number of board memberships per person

"The number of directorship responsibilities on various boards by one board member should be limited (to about 5)."				
	Agree	Disagree	Depends	Blank
Board of directors	2/7	2/7	3/7	0/7
Executive Committee	11/14	3/14	0/14	0/14
Capital providers	7/9	2/9	0/9	0/9
External auditors	7/11	4/11	0/11	0/11
Academics	7/8	0/8	0/8	1/8

Between the board members and the other parties, a remarkable rift of opinions is revealed in Table 12: while most other parties tend to agree – not unanimously, it is to be admitted – that one person cannot collect too large a number of these mandates, few board members themselves think this way. An academic argues that a directorship can take up quite a bit of time, even in small companies. Similarly, investors and executives agree that if the board member wants to take the job seriously, he/she should limit the number of mandates.

This finishes the Table Round's discussions of the first theme, the Board of Directors. The next group of issues relate to the audit committee, to which we turn in Chapter 2.

4. CONCLUSIONS

In this chapter we first looked at the empirical evidence *re* effective corporate boards, then provide a summary of the points of view of our round-table participants in this matter, and finally provide some statistics regarding Belgian practices. From the empirical evidence we learn that there is no unanimous support for the hypothesis that certain board characteristics are more effective than others. It is often suggested (by policymakers) that board effectiveness is negatively associated with board size and positively with board independence. The evidence regarding board size is generally (although not fully) consistent with this suggestion. However, as far as board independence is concerned, there is no evidence that this leads to better (accounting) performance or corporate decisions. Some studies even report a negative association between board independence and accounting performance, and there is also no clear association between board independence and the quality of decision making in an acquisition context. Also, independent boards do not always lead to prompter dismissal of badly performing CEO'S. The evidence does however support the hypothesis that board independence is associated with less earnings management and fraudulent companies have (on average) less independent boards. From the latter result one should, however, not necessarily conclude that the inclusion of outside members on the board of directors could increase the board's effectiveness at monitoring management for the prevention of financial statement fraud. It is, indeed, also possible that managers that are more prone to commit fraud also fight harder against the inclusion of independent board members, so that manager fraud propensity drives both the likelihood of fraud and the degree of board independence.

The opinions of the round-table participants generally do not deviate that much from the empirical findings. A vast majority of (or in some case all) participants believes that boards should be kept small in size and that board characteristics potentially have an impact on financial statement fraud and on the quality of the financial statement information. But there is no consensus that independent boards would lead to better performance or better decisions, such for example in an acquisition context or the dismissal of poorly performing CEO's.

Finally, we also investigated the actual board practices of a sample of Belgian listed companies, and find that the median board in our sample consists of 9 members, on 40% of these are independent. In a vast majority of cases, that is on average 65-70% of companies, the roles of CEO and chairman are split.

REFERENCES

Abbott, L.J., S. Parker and G.F. Peters. 2002. *Audit committee characteristics and financial misstatement: A Study of the Efficacy of Certain Blue Ribbon Committee Recommendations.* Working paper.

Agrawal, A., and C. Knoeber. 1996. Firm performance and mechanisms to control agency problems between managers and shareholders. *Journal of Financial and Quantitative Analysis* 31: 377-396.

Agrawal, A. and C. Sahiba. 2003. *Who is Afraid of Reg FD? The Behavior and Performance of Sell-Side Analysts Following the SEC's Fair Disclosure Rules.* AFA 2003 Washington, DC Meetings; EFA 2002 Berlin Meetings Presented

Antle, R. and A. Smith. 1986. An Empirical Investigation of the Relative Performance Evaluation of Corporate Executives. *Journal of Accounting Research* 24(1): 1-39.

Baliga, B.R., R.C. Moyer and R.S. Rao. 1996. CEO duality and firm performance: What's the fuss? *Strategic Management Journal 17*: 41-53.

Beasley, M. S. 1996. An empirical analysis of the relation between the board of director composition and financial statement fraud. *The Accounting Review* 71: 443 465.

Bhagat, S. and B. Black. 1999. The Uncertain Relationship between Board Composition and Firm Performance. *Business Lawyer* 54: 921-963.

Bhagat, S. and B. Black. 2000. *Board Independence and Long-Term Firm Performance.* Working Paper, University of Colorado.

Bhagat, S. and B. Black. 2001. The Non-Correlation Between Board Independence and Long Term Firm Performance. *Journal of Corporation Law* 27: 231-274.

Borokhovich, K.A., R. Parrino and T. Trapani. 1996, Outside directors and CEO selection, *Journal of Financial and Quantitative Analysis* 31, 337-355.

Brickley, J., S. Bhagat and R. Lease. 1985. The Impact of Long-range Managerial Compensation Plans on Shareholder Wealth. *Journal of Accounting and Economics* 7: 115-29.

Brickley, J., J. Coles and R. Terry. 1994. Outside directors and the adoption of poison pills. *Journal of Financial Economics* 35: 371-332.

Brickley, J.A., J.L. Coles and G. Jarrell. 1997. Leadership structure: Separating the CEO and Chairman of the Board. *Journal of Corporate Finance* 3: 189-220.

Byrd, J. and K. Hickman. 1992. Do Outside Directors Monitor Managers? Evidence from Tender Offer Bids. *Journal of Financial Economics*, 32, pp. 195-207.

Cadbury Report. 1992. *Report of the Committee on the Financial Aspects of Corporate Governance*. London: Gee & Co.

Chaganti, R. S., V. Mahajan, and S. Sharma. 1985. Corporate Board Size, Composition and Corporate Failures in Retailing Industry. *Journal of Management Studies* 22: 400 (1985).

Conyon, M. and K. Murphy. 2000. The prince and the pauper: CEO pay in the United States and United Kingdom. *Economic Journal* 110: 640-671.

Core, J., R. Holthausen and D. Larcker. 1999. Corporate Governance, Chief Executive Officer Compensation, and Firm Performance. *Journal of Financial Economics* 51: 371-406.

Core, J. and D. Larcker. 2001. *Performance Consequences of Mandatory Increases in CEO Stock Ownership*. Working paper, University of Pennsylvania.

Cotter, J., A. Shivdasani, and M. Zenner. 1997. Do Independent Directors Enhance Target Shareholder Wealth during Tender Offers? *Journal of Financial Economics* 43: 195-218.

Dechow, P.M., R.G. Sloan, and A.P. Sweeney. 1996. Causes and Consequences of Earnings Manipulations: Analysis of Firms Subject to Enforcement Action by SEC, *Contemporary Accounting Research* (Spring): 1-36.

Degeorge, F., J. Patel and R. Zeckhauser. 1999. Earnings management to exceed thresholds. *Journal of Business* 27: 1-33.

Demsetz, H. and K. Lehn. 1985. The Structure of Corporate Ownership: Causes and Consequences. *Journal of Political Economy* 93: 1155-1177.

Denis, D.K. and A. Sarin. 1999. Ownership and Board Structures in Publicly Traded Corporations. *Journal of Financial Economics* 52: 187-224.

Denis, D.K. 2001. Twenty-five Years of Corporate Governance Research ...and Counting. *Review of Financial Economics* 10: 191-212.

Denis, D.K. and J.J. McConnell. 2003. International Corporate Governance. *Journal of Financial and Quantitative Analysis* 38 (1): 1-36.

Eisenberg, T., S. Sundgren, and M.T. Wells. "Larger Board Size and Decreasing Firm Value in Small Firms," *Journal of Financial Economics*, 48 (1998), 35-54.

Fama, E. F. and M. C. Jensen. 1983. Agency Problems and Residual Claims. *Journal of Law and Economics* 26, no. 2: 327-349.

Franks, J., C. Mayer, and L. Renneboog. 2001. Who Disciplines Managers in Poorly Performing Companies? *Journal of Financial Intermediation* 10: 209-248.

Gaver, J. J., K. M. Gaver and J. R. Austin. 1995. Additional evidence on bonus plans and income management. *Journal of Accounting and Economics* 19: 3-28.

Goyal, V.K. and C.W. Park. 2002. Board Leadership Structure and CEO Turnover. *Journal of Corporate Finance* 8 (1): 49-66.

Guay, W.R., J.E. Core and D.F. Larcker. 2002. *Executive Equity Compensation and Incentives: A Survey* (January 9, 2002). http://ssrn.com/abstract=276425

Hall, B., and J. Liebman. 1998. Are CEOs really paid like bureaucrats? *The Quarterly Journal of Economics* 103: 653-691.

Hall, B. and K. Murphy. 2000. *Stock Options for Undiversified Executives.* Working paper, Harvard University.

Hambrick D.C. and E.M. Jackson. 2000. Outside Directors with a Stake: The Linchpin in Improving Governance. *California Managment Review* 42 (4): 108-127.

Healy, P. M. 1985. The effects of bonus schemes on accounting decisions, *Journal of Accounting and Economics* 7: 85-107.

Healy, P. M. and K. Palepu. 1995. The challenges of investor communication. *Journal of Financial Economics* 38: 111-140.

Hermalin, B. E. and M. S. Weisbach. 1998. Endogenously Chosen Board of Directors and Their Monitoring of the CEO, *The American Economic Review* 96 (1998).

Hermalin, B.E. and M.S. Weisbach. 2003. Boards of Directors as an Endogenously Determined Institution: A Survey of the Economic Literature. *Economic Policy Review* (April): 6-27.

Himmelberg, C., R. Hubbard and D. Palia. 1999. Understanding the determinants of managerial ownership and the link between ownership and performance. *Journal of Financial Economics* 53: 353-384.

Hirshleifer, D., and A. Thakor. 1994. Managerial Performance, Boards of Directors, and Takeover Bidding. *Journal of Corporate Finance* 1: 63-90.

Holderness, C.G. and D.P. Sheehan. 1988. The role of majority shareholders in publicly held corporations: An exploratory analysis, *Journal of Financial Economics* 20: 317-346.

Holderness, C.G., 2003, A Survey of Blockholders and Corporate Control. *Economic Policy Review* (April): 50-65.

Holthausen, R. W., Larcker, D., Sloan, R., 1995. Annual bonus schemes and the manipulation of earnings. *Journal of Accounting and Economics* 19, 29-74.

Jensen, M. C. and W. Meckling. 1976. The Theory of the Firm: Managerial Behavior, Agency Costs and Ownership Structure. *Journal of Financial Economics* 3: 305-360.

Jensen, M. and K. Murphy. 1990. Performance pay and top-management incentives. *Journal of Political Economy* 98: 225-264.

Jensen, M. C. 1993. The modern industrial revolution, exit, and the failure of internal control systems. *Journal of Finance*, 48, 831–880.

Kang, J. and A. Shivdasani. 1995. Firm Performance, Corporate Governance, and Top Executive Turnover in Japan. *Journal of Financial Economics* 38(1): 29-58.

Kaplan, S. 1994. Top Executives, Turnover, and Firm Performance in Germany. *Journal of Law, Economics, and Organization* 10: 142-159.

Kaplan, S.N. and B.A. Minton. 1994. Appointments of outsiders to Japanese boards: Determinants and implications for managers. *Journal of Financial Economics* 36: 225-257.

Klein, A. 1998. Firm performance and board committee Structure. *Journal of Law and Economics* 41, 274-303.

Klein, A. 2000. *CEO power, board independence and CEO compensation: An empirical investigation*. Working paper, New York University.

McConnell, J.J. and H. Servaes. 1990. Additional evidence on equity ownership and corporate value. *Journal of Financial Economics* 27: 595-612.

Milliron, J. 2000. *Board of Director Incentive Alignment and the Design of Executive Compensation Contracts*. Unpublished dissertation thesis, University of Chicago.

Morck, R., A. Shleifer and R. Vishny. 1988. Management Ownership and Market Valuation: An Empirical Analysis. *Journal of Financial Economics* 20: 293-316.

Murphy, K. 1999. Executive Compensation, in Ed. O Ashenfelter and D. Card, *Handbook of Labor Economics*, Vol. III, Amsterdam: North-Holland, 2485-2563.

Peasnell, K.V., P.F. Pope and S. Young. 2000. Detecting earnings management using cross-sectional abnormal accrual models. *Accounting ad Business Research* 30: 303-326.

Perry, T. 2000. *Incentive Compensation for Outside Directors and CEO Turnover*. Working paper, Arizona State University.

Pi, L. and S.G. Timme. 1993. Corporate control and bank efficiency. *Journal of Banking and Finance* 17: 515-530.

Rechner I. F. and D. R. Dalton. 1991. CEO duality and organizational performance: A longitudinal analysis. *Strategic Management Journal* 12: 155-160.

Renneboog, L. 2000 Ownership, Managerial Control and the Corporate Governance of Companies Listed on the Brussels Stock Exchange. *Journal of Banking and Finance* 24: 1959-1995.

Rodriguez, E.F. and S.G. Anson. 2001. *Wealth Effects Associated with the Compliance with the Code of Best Practice: The Spanish Experience.* Working Paper.

Rosenstein, S. and J.G. Wyatt. 1990. Outside directors, board independence and stockholder wealth. *Journal of Financial Economics* 26, 175-191.

Schipper, K., 1989. Earnings management. *Accounting Horizons* 3: 91-102.

Shivdasani, A. and D.L. Yermack. 1999. CEO involvement in the selection of new board members: An empirical analysis. *Journal of Finance* 54, 1829-1853.

Smith, C. and R. Watts. 1992. The Investment Opportunity Set and Corporate Financing, Dividend and Compensation Policies. *Journal of Financial Economics* 32: 263-292.

Subrahmanyam V., N. Rangan, and S. Rosenstein. 1997. The role of outside directors in bank acquisitions. *Financial Management* 26: 23-36.

Vafeas, N. and E. Theodorou. 1998. The Association Between Board Structure and Firm Performance in the UK. *British Accounting Review* 30: 383-407.

Weisbach, M. 1988. Outside Directors and CEO Turnover. *Journal of Financial Economics* 20: 431-460.

Yermack, D. 1996. Higher market valuation of companies with a small board of directors, *Journal of Financial Economics* 40, 185-211.

Yermack, D. 1997. Good Timing: CEO Stock Option Awards and Company News Announcements. *Journal of Finance* 52(2): 449-476

CHAPTER 2
THE AUDIT COMMITTEE

The audit committee is a subcommittee of the board of directors, without executive powers, which oversees the internal and external audit processes of the firm. The audit committee is expected to maintain a continuing review of the corporation's financial data and to ensure that the firm has adequate internal controls, appropriate accounting policies, and external auditors who deter fraud and promote high-quality and timely financial statements. The committee achieves this goal by recommending the external auditor to shareholders, and by interfacing with the external auditors, the internal auditors, and the board of directors.

In a world without agency costs there would be no need for an audit committee. In reality, however, such a committee may reduce the agency problem by facilitating the timely release of unbiased, accounting information by managers to stakeholders of the company, thus reducing the information asymmetry between insiders and outsiders (Klein, 1998).

There are two potential monitoring advantages to be gained from assigning the general board's oversight responsibilities to a board committee: independence and board efficiency. First, the independence and integrity of monitoring may be enhanced by having both internal and external auditors report to a subset of the board that consists of outside directors. Second, board committees can help improve the efficiency of board functioning as it can investigate problems in greater depth and detail than an entire board. The successful functioning of an audit committee depends very much on two important characteristics: independence and competence.

Independence and the effectiveness of the audit committee

Independence is considered an essential quality for an audit committee to fulfil its oversight role. This explains why stock exchanges have rules and regulations regarding audit-committee independence. The NYSE's corporate governance Standards issued as Section 303A and approved by the SEC in November 2003 require that all audit committee members satisfy the requirements for independence set out in the standards. Note that the issue of independence was already promoted by the Blue Ribbon Committee in 1999: "several recent studies have produced a correlation between audit committee independence and two desirable outcomes: a higher degree of active oversight and a lower incidence of financial statement fraud. (BRC; 1999,

p. 22)" If independence results in better oversight, audit committee independence is expected to be associated with lower levels of earnings management and financial-statement fraud. In December 1999 the NYSE and NASDAQ accordingly modified the requirements for audit committees for all listed, large U.S. companies. Under the new standards, firms must maintain audit committees comprised of three or more directors who have no relationship to the company that may interfere with the exercise of their independence from management and the company.

The BRC (1999) likewise recommended that the audit committee should be comprised only of outside directors. Since independent audit committee members are not associated with management, they may be better positioned to perform their oversight role and motivate external auditors to be impartial. Furthermore, by being financially independent of management, independent directors should be better able to withstand pressure from the firm to manipulate earnings. Improved monitoring by independent directors is expected to result from incentives for such directors to build and maintain reputations as decision-control experts (Fama and Jensen, 1983). Although audit committee service may increase a director's reputation as a monitor, it also exacerbates the potential reputational damage should a financial misstatement occur while the director serves on the audit committee. Consequently, the preservation of reputational capital serves as one motivation for higher-quality monitoring on the part of outside, independent directors. It could be argued that being an outsider is not enough, in this respect: the member should also be not a manager. Notably, if audit committee members are themselves managers of another company, they may be less inclined to criticize the firm's management.

Competence

Because of its responsibility for overseeing internal control and financial reporting, a well-functioning audit committee needs not just independence but also a certain level of financial competence. Accordingly, in the US the NYSE's corporate governance standards for listed issuers (as approved by the SEC in 2003) require that listed companies have an audit committee that satisfies the requirements of Rule 10A-3 under the Exchange Act. This implies, amongst other things, that the audit committee must have at least three members and each member must be financially literate. Note that requirement is not entirely new as the Blue Ribbon Committee (BRC, 1999) already in 1999 recommended that each member of the audit committee should be or become financially literate and that at least one member should have accounting or related financial management expertise. The Blue Ribbon Committee (1999, p. 25) defines financial expertise as "past employment experience in finance or accounting, requisite professional certification in accounting, or any other comparable experience or background which results in the individual's financial sophistication, including being or having been a CEO or other senior officer with financial oversight responsibilities". Financial expertise increases the likelihood that the audit committee is able to recognize potentially misleading transactions or financial statements and contribute to high-quality reporting. Note that Section 407 of the Sarbanes-Oxley Act (2002) requires disclosure about the fact that at least one member of an issuer (i.e. stock-listed company) is a financial expert.

Audit committees in Europe

Audit committee installation, independence and competence, has also been the subject of debate by European corporate governance regulators and policymakers. Although the importance of audit committees is well recognized in Europe and the principles are nowadays similar to those in the US, is there one huge difference still: the standards are not mandatory. Given that European corporate governance rules are to be applied by listed companies on a "comply or explain" basis, is deviation from best practice always possible if motivated and explained (for further details see also chapter 7).

Before reporting the debates at our Table Round, we first present a review of the extant literature.

1. RELATED RESEARCH

a. IMPACT OF THE AUDIT COMMITTEE ON EARNINGS MANAGEMENT

If audit-committee independence leads to better oversight, we should observe lower levels of earnings management. Consistently with this prediction, DeFond and Jiambalvo (1991) find that earnings overstatements are less prevalent for firms that have audit committees. Klein (2002) finds that there is a non-linear negative relationship between audit committee independence and earnings management. Specifically, a significant relation is found only when the audit committee has less than a majority of independent directors. No significant association is found between earnings management and the more stringent requirement of 100% audit committee independence; in light of this, the Blue Ribbon Committee's recommendation may have overshot its mark.

b. IMPACT ON EXTERNAL AUDITOR OPINION

According to the extant literature (*e.g.*, Antle and Nalebuff 1991; Knapp 1985), the issuance of a going-concern audit opinion[5] can be considered as the outcome of an often contentious negotiation among management, the auditor, and the audit committee. The difficulty and ambiguity in the going-concern reporting decision may render the auditor susceptible to management pressure. For example, clients receiving a going-concern report may be more likely to switch auditors. An independent audit committee could help mitigate such pressure by supporting the auditor in disputes with management (McMullen 1996; Parker, 2000).

As expected on the basis of the above, Carcello and Neal (2000) find a significantly negative relationship between the percentage of affiliated (gray and inside) directors on the audit committee and the likelihood of financially distressed firms receiving a going-concern audit qualification. Specifically, their results suggest that auditors are less likely to modify the reports of distressed companies that have a greater percentage of affiliated directors on their audit committees. These findings suggest that explicitly conferring auditor-engagement rights on the audit committee may further increase the auditor's ability to withstand management pressures, potentially resulting in less aggressive accounting and/or more thorough audit procedures. But, again, an alternative explanation is that distressed companies (where going-concern reports are more frequent) may also be more likely to attract outside directors.

c. IMPACT ON FINANCIAL MISSTATEMENTS AND FRAUD

The audit committee is expected to ensure that the firm has appropriate accounting policies, adequate internal control and external auditors who deter fraud and promote high-quality and timely financial statements. McMullen (1996) and Dechow, Sloan, and Sweeney (1996) find evidence that firms committing financial fraud are less likely to have audit committees at the time of the fraud than other firms. Beasley (1996), on the other hand, finds no relationship between the incidence of financial-statement fraud and the existence of an audit committee.

Other studies ask the question as to what characteristics make an audit committee more effective, and support the BRC's hunch that audit-committee independence and expertise are both important factors. Abbott *et al.* (2002) and Felo *et al.* (2003) document that financial misstatements are less likely to occur in firms with audit committees that are independent and that have a financial expert. Beasley (1996)

5 An auditor who believes that a company is about to fail is required to signal this to investors by giving a going-concern qualification in the audit report.

obtains similar results, finding the percentage of outside directors on the audit committee to be lower for firms that committed financial statement fraud. In another study, Beasley *et al.* (2000) investigate fraudulent financial reporting in the technology, health care and financial-services industries. They find that in these industries, firms committing fraud have less independent audit committees and boards.

2. ACTUAL PRACTICE IN BELGIUM

a. DESCRIPTIVE STATISTICS

Recall, from Table 4, that about three companies out of four do use an audit committee, and that fixed compensation is adopted virtually everywhere (a laudable and logical practice). Our survey revealed that, in Belgium, about three listed companies out of four have an audit committee, and that the typical audit committee has 2.3 members and meets 3.6 times a year.

b. EFFECTIVENESS OF AUDIT COMMITTEE: EVIDENCE FOR BELGIUM

In this sub-section we report the results of the estimation of two empirical models using the Belgian data we collected. The first model relates to earnings management and the second model to voluntary disclosure or transparency. These results were also presented at the round table sessions.

Audit committee existence and earnings management

We have estimated the following earnings-management model:

Earnings management = f (governance variables, control variables)

The choice of both the governance and control variables is consistent with prior research studies on determinants of earnings management. Table 13 provides a summary of the results. Note that earnings management is not observable, and needs to be assessed using a proxy. A simple but popular proxy in the literature is the absolute value of unexpected accruals. Unexpected accruals are proxied by the change in the accruals as compared to previous year.

Table 13: Association of governance characteristics and earnings management

Variable	coefficient	p-value
Intercept	0.41005	< 0.0001
Test variables:		
Board size	-0.02586	<0.10
CEO = CHAIR (yes = 1)	-0,10503	<0.05
BoD has charter	-0,10063	<0.05
% non-executives BoD	0,01790	n.s.
Audit Committee	0,06623	n.s.
Control variables:		
LT Debtratio	-0,55946	<0.01
Manufacturing	-0,02987	n.s.
Technology	0,15318	<0.01
ROE	0,16088	<0.05
EQ/TA	-0,32505	<0.05

Adj R^2 = 44,42%, p-value model 0,0002

Note that five governance variables were tested: board size, CEO and chairman, presence of a board charter, percentage of non-executive directors and the presence of an audit committee. Control variables are variables that need to be included in the model, as they have proven to affect the degree of earnings management in prior research studies. They include: leverage (measured as long term debt divided by total assets), industry membership variables, return on equity and equity divided total assets.

In the second column of Table 13 we report the estimated coefficients for the test and control variables. A negative coefficient indicates a negative association between the variable and earnings management, whereas a positive coefficient represents a positive association with earnings management. The third column provides the p-values. If a parameter has a p-value smaller than 0.10, this indicates that the estimated association between the variable and earnings management is probably not attributable to chance. The smaller the p number, the less likely it is that the estimated relation is just a fluke that would disappear in a sufficiently large sample.

Table 13 indicates no significant association between the existence of an audit committee and earnings management. As far as we can tell from the 2001 sample, audit committees may not have been effective in constraining earnings management in Belgium.

Audit committee existence and transparency

We have estimated the following transparency model:

Transparency = f (governance variables, control variables)

The choice of both the governance and control variables is consistent with prior research studies on determinants of voluntary disclosure or transparency (see also Chapter 5 for an overview). Transparency is measured based on the ValueReporting™ model and framework by PricewaterhouseCoopers (see also chapter 6 for more details). Table 14 provides a summary of the results.

Table 14

Variable	Coefficient	p-value
Intercept	-51,61490	<0,05
Governance variables:		
Number meetings BOD	-2,27347	< 0,01
Big 4	10,19387	0,1366
Audit committee	-3,35647	n.s.
Control variables:		
LNASSET	7,23763	<0,0001
PEmultiple	0,17167	<0,10
EQ/TA	27,95096	<0,05
ROE	16,87255	<0,05
Manufacturing	1,83566	n.s.
Technology	-11,42644	<0,10

Adj R^2 = 45,7%; p-value model < 0,0001

Table 14 reveals no significant association between the existence of an audit committee and corporate transparency. However, there seems to be a statistically clear association between audit type and transparency. The results suggest that companies that appoint a big 4 auditor are more transparent, ceteris paribus.

3. ROUND-TABLE SESSION

In general, the audit committee is viewed as very useful in boosting the efficiency of the board when it seeks answers and solutions to very specific questions and problems.

Capital providers assert that the main task of the audit committee should be to assure the reliability of the information provided to the board and, in a later stage, to the investors. It is surely more difficult for the entire board to investigate problems in great depth and detail than it is for the audit committee. Only in a small firm with a small board an audit committee will probably not be needed.

But some board members are far less convinced that an audit committee can increase board's efficiency. One of them argues that, all too often, working in committees creates more scope for manipulation and below-the-table deals; instead, the whole board should take responsibility. Other board members reply that it is not very efficient that a large board do all the work itself. In addition, the argument that the whole board should take responsibility is not to the point: the board always takes the final decision already and bears the final responsibility anyway, as committees perform an advisory role only.

To what extent do audit committees reduce fraud in a firm?

Executives argue that public trust is based on the integrity of the firm's functioning and that the audit committee plays an important role in enforcing that certain procedures be followed. The fundamental question in fraud prevention is not: "how well does your audit committee work", but "how well do your systems work". The key to effectively rein in fraud is that people in different positions are conscious of the business-policy rules within the firm and commit themselves to it. But this view is not shared by all, as Table 15 shows.

Table 15: Audit committees and fraud prevention

"Audit committees are ineffective in preventing financial statement fraud."				
	Agree	Disagree	Depends	Blank
Board of directors	2/7	4/7	1/7	0/7
Executive Committee	5/14	8/14	0/14	1/14
Capital providers	2/9	6/9	1/9	0/9
External auditors	2/11	9/11	0/11	0/11
Academics	2/8	6/8	0/8	0/8

Executives and capital providers agree that there is a tendency to shift responsibilities from boards to the audit committee, and not to the external audit. A capital provider states that Belgian law does not recognize this shift and that the board still retains the final responsibility. Auditors agree: the audit committee has an advisory task only. But a capital provider replies that other forces are at work, namely the moral hazard issue, where everyone wants to be covered. The board feels safer if it has set up an audit committee.

Should audit-committee members be fully independent?

Table 16: Composition of audit committees

"Audit committees should consist 100% of independent members."				
	Agree	Disagree	Depends	Blank
Board of directors	4/7	3/7	0/7	0/7
Executive Committee	2/14	12/14	0/14	0/14
Capital providers	3/9	5/9	1/9	0/9
External auditors	7/11	4/11	0/11	0/11
Academics	4/8	4/8	0/8	0/8

Both capital providers and academics argue that the audit committee should be to a large extent composed of independent members. But they add that one should not over-emphasize the "independence" issue. In itself, independence will not do the job: integrity, ability and knowledge of the members and the quality of information supplied to the committee are at least equally important.

Should at least half of the audit committee members be financial experts?

There is a wide consensus that financial literacy is very important for audit committee members, but should not be required for each and every board member. Auditors and board members add that, in the current public mood and legal environment, people are not keen on being *the* financial expert of the audit committee because of the potentially heavy responsibilities that come with this function. An academic argues that the board should be made legally liable for appointing financial illiterates to the audit committee: such a decision would fall under gross negligence.

Table 17: Financial expertise in the audit committee

"At least half of the audit committee members should be financial experts."				
	Agree	Disagree	Depends	Blank
Board of directors	3/7	3/7	1/7	0/7
Executive Committee	11/14	3/14	0/14	0/14
Capital providers	8/9	0/9	1/9	0/9
External auditors	7/11	4/11	0/11	0/11
Academics	8/8	0/8	0/8	0/8

After our discussion of the Board and its (internal) Audit Committee, we now turn to a second internal function, very much related to public trust and governance: the internal audit.

4. CONCLUSIONS

In this chapter we first looked at the empirical evidence *re* effectiveness of audit committees, then gave an overview of the points of view of the round-table session in this matter, and finally provided some statistics regarding Belgian practices. The extant empirical evidence supports to a large extent the hypothesis that audit committees are effective governance mechanisms. In particular, the empirical results suggest that audit-committee independence is negatively associated with earnings management, or with receiving a going-concern opinion and committing financial statement fraud. However, these strong empirical results do not seem to convince all round table participants of the effectiveness of audit committees in constraining earnings management and preventing fraud.

We also report some evidence for Belgium. Although three out of four companies have set up an audit committee, our sample provides no statistically clear evidence that these committees are indeed effective: our multiple-regression analyses do not reveal a significant constraining effect of audit committee existence on earnings management. Also, there is no unambiguous association between audit-committee existence and corporate transparency. Note however the exploratory nature of our tests. The sample is small, and unlike the American studies we do not have data on audit-committee characteristics; we just test the mere existence of an audit committee. If, in reality, only audit committees with independent and competerent members are effective, then a test that ignores this distinction may incorrectly conclude that audit committees are ineffective across the board.

REFERENCES

Abbott, L.J., and S. Parker. 2000. Auditor selection and audit committee characteristics. *Auditing: A Journal of Practice and Theory*. 19 (2): 47-66.

Abbott, L.J., S. Parker, and G.F. Peters. 2002. *Audit committee characteristics and financial misstatement: A Study of the Efficacy of Certain Blue Ribbon Committee Recommendations*. Working paper.

Antle, R., and B. Nalebuff. 1991. Conservatism and auditor-client negotiations. *Journal of Accounting Research* 29 (Supplement): 31-54.

Beasley, M.S. 1996. An empirical analysis of the relation between board of director composition and financial statement fraud. *The Accounting Review* 71 (4): 443-465.

Beasley, M., Carcello, J. V., Hermanson, D. and P. Lapides. 2000. Fraudulent financial reporting: Consideration of industry traits and corporate governance mechanisms. *Accounting Horizons*, Vol. 14, No. 4 (December): 441 – 454.

Blue Ribbon Committee (BRC). 1999. *Report and Recommendations of the Blue Ribbon Committee on Improving the Effectiveness of Corporate Audit Committees.* New York, NY: New York Stock Exchange and National Association of Securities Dealers.

Bradbury, M. 1990. The incentives for voluntary audit committee formation. *Journal of Accounting and Public Policy* 9: 19-36.

Cadbury Committee.1992. *Report of The Committee on The Financial Aspects of Corporate Governance.* Londen: Gee.

Carcello, J. and T. Neal. 2000. Audit committee characteristics and auditor reporting. *The Accounting Review* 75 (4): 453 – 467.

Chow, C. W., and S. J. Rice. 1982. Qualified audit opinions and auditor switching. *The Accounting Review* 57 (April): 326-335.

Collier, P. 1993. Factors affecting the formation of audit committees in major UK listed companies. *Accounting and Business Research* 23: 421-430.

Dechow, P.M., R.G. Sloan, and A.P. Sweeney. 1996. Causes and consequences of earnings manipulations: An analysis of firms subject to enforcement actions by the SEC. *Contemporary Accounting Research.* (Spring): 1-36.

DeFond, M. L. and J. Jiambalvo. 1991. Incidence and circumstances of accounting errors. *The Accounting Review* 66 (July): 643-655.

Deli, D.N. and S.L. Gillan. 2000. On the demand for independent and active audit committees. *Journal of Corporate Finance* 6: 427-445.

DeZoort, F.T. and S.E. Salterio. 2001. The effects of corporate governance experience and financial-reporting and audit knowledge on audit committee members' judgment. *Auditing: A Journal of Practice and Theory.* 20 (2): 31-47.

Eichenseher, J. W. and D. Shields. 1985. Corporate director liability and monitoring preferences. *Journal of Accounting and Public Policy* 4: 13-31.

Fama, E. F., and M. C. Jensen. 1983. Separation of ownership and control *Journal of Law and Economics* 26: 301-325.

Felo, A.J., S. Krishnamurthy and S.A. Solieri. 2003. *Audit Committee Characteristics and the Perceived Quality of Financial Reporting: An Empirical Analysis.* Working Paper.

Jensen, M.C. 1993. The modern industrial revolution, exit and the failure of internal control systems. *Journal of Finance* 48 (3): 831-880.

Jensen, M. C., and W. H. Meckling. 1977. Theory of the firm: Managerial behavior, agency costs and ownership structure. *Journal of Financial Economics* 3: 305-360.

Klein, A. 1998. Firm performance and board committee structure. *Journal of Law and Economics* 41: 275-303.

Klein, A. 2002. Audit committee, board of director characteristics, and earnings management. *Journal of Accounting and Economics.* 33 (3): 375-400.

Knapp, M. C. 1985. Audit conflict: An empirical study of the perceived ability of auditors to resist management pressure. *The Accounting Review* 60 (April): 202-211.

Mizruchi, M.S. 1983. Who controls whom? An examination of the relation between management and board of directors of large American corporations. *Academy of Management Review* 8 (3): 426-435.

McMullen, D. A. 1996. Audit committee performance: An investigation of the consequences associated with audit committees. *Auditing: A Journal of Practice and Theory* 15 (Spring): 87-103.

Menon, K., and J. D. Williams. 1994. The use of audit committees for monitoring. *Journal of Accounting and Public Policy* 13: 121-139.

Parker, S. 2000. *The association between audit committee characteristics and the conservatism of financial reporting*. Working paper, Santa Clara University.

Pincus, K., M. Rusbarsky, and J. Wong. 1989. Voluntary formation of corporate audit committees among NASDAQ firms, *Journal of Accounting and Public Policy* 8, 239-265.

Piot, C. 2001. Agency costs and audit quality: evidence from France. *The European Accounting Review* 10 (3): 461-499.

Raghunandan, K., W.J. Read, and D.V. Rama. 2001. Audit committee composition, "Gray Directors," and interaction with internal auditing. *Accounting Horizons* 15 (2): 105-118.

Scarbrough, D. P., D. V. Rama, and K. Raghunandan. 1998. Audit committee composition and interaction with internal auditing: Canadian evidence. *Accounting Horizons* 12 (March): 51-62.

Vafeas, N. 2000. Board structure and the informativeness of earnings. *Journal of Accounting and Public Policy,* 19: 139-160.

Watts, R.L., and J.L. Zimmerman. 1986. Positive Accounting Theory. *Englewood Cliffs, NJ: Prentice-Hall.*

CHAPTER 3
THE INTERNAL AUDIT, INTERNAL CONTROL AND RISK MANAGEMENT

Mid-2002, in response to the familiar financial disastersthe Sarbanes-Oxley Act and other new exchange listing proposals were passed to help restore investor confidence. Section 404 of the Sarbanes-Oxley Act requires that management assesses the internal controls in the corporation, and issues an internal control report. Another new requirement was that listed companies have an effective internal-audit function. In addition, the Sarbanes-Oxley Act of 2002 stops the external auditor from taking up certain outsourced activities, including internal-audit services – a common method for providing internal-auditing services to family businesses (Carey *et al.*; 2001).

Internal control and risk management

The importance of internal control processes is emphasized by the exposure draft on *Enterprise Risk Management* issued in 2003 by the Committee of Sponsoring Organizations of the Treadway Commission (COSO). This draft builds on the 1992 COSO report on internal control and provides guidance on sound control and risk management practices.

The 2003 COSO report on enterprise risk management builds on the 1992 guidelines on internal control and defines enterprise risk management as:

> "*... a process, effected by an entity's board of directors, management and other personnel, applied in strategy setting and across in the enterprise, designed to identify potential events that may affect the entity, and manage risks to be within its risk appetite, to provide reasonable assurance regarding the achievement of entity objectives.*"

There are four objectives related to internal control:
- To understand the extent to which the entity's strategic objectives are being achieved.
- To understand the extent to which the entity's operating objectives are being achieved.
- To determine that the entity's reporting is reliable.
- To determine that applicable laws and regulations are being complied with.

COSO/ERM Framework 2003

INTERNAL ENVIRONMENT: – Risk management philosophy – Risk culture – Board of directors – Integrity and ethical values – Commitment to competence – Management's Philosophy and Operating style – Risk appetite – Organizational structure – Assignment of authority and responsibility – Human resources policies and practices
OBJECTIVE SETTING: – Strategic objectives – Related objectives – Selected objectives – Risk appetite – Risk tolerance
EVENT IDENTIFICATION: – Events – Factors influencing strategy and objectives – Methodologies and techniques – Event interdependencies – Event categories – Risks and opportunities
RISK ASSESSMENT: – Inherent and residual risk – Likelihood and impact – Methodologies and techniques – correlation
RISK RESPONSE: – Identify risk responses – Evaluate possible risk responses – Select responses – Portfolio view
CONTROL ACTIVITIES: – Integration with risk response – Types of control activities – General controls – Application controls – Entity specific
INFORMATION AND COMMUNICATION: – Information – Strategy and integrated systems – communication
MONITORING: – Separate evaluations – Ongoing evaluations

Internal control and risk management include all measures and practices that are used to mitigate exposures to risks that could potentially prevent an organization from achieving its objectives (Knechel, 2002). It also serves as the first line of defence in safeguarding assets and preventing and detecting errors and *fraud*. Internal control is not solely a procedure or policy that is performed at a certain point in time, but rather it is an ongoing process operating at multiple levels within an organization. The COSO framework (2003) identifies and describes the following components necessary for effective risk management:

1. Internal environment
2. Objective setting
3. Event identification
4. Risk assessment
5. Risk response
6. Control activities
7. Information and communications
8. Monitoring

Internal auditing

The recent corporate governance best-practice codes (for example, the Lippens Code in Belgium) very explicitly recommend the installation of an internal audit function in listed companies. Internal auditing is an independent, objective assurance and consulting activity designed to improve an organisation's operations and, thus, to add value. It helps an organisation accomplish its objectives by bringing a systematic, disciplined approach to evaluate and improve the effectiveness of risk-management, control, and governance processes. (IIA, The Institute of Internal Auditors)

A first objective of the internal audit is to provide assurance that the risk-management processes are functioning as intended. Through specific recommendations and other consulting services, the internal-audit function furthermore assists management and the board by improving risk-management and control processes. Internal auditors should be, or become, very familiar with an organization's value creation, as they accumulate knowledge about the organization throughout their careers; they can therefore be ideal consultants for the improvement of an organization's processes. The improvement of internal processes is likely to have a positive effect on suppliers and customers (*e.g.*, cost savings, reduced production times, improved quality of products); thus, the internal-audit function is also able to add value to external parties.

In addition, an internal auditor's monitoring can reduce the risk that management overrides internal controls or that employees circumvent them. Employees may be more conscientious about performing control policies and procedures if they know their work is being monitored. Breakdowns in internal control can be detected on a more timely basis by an effective internal auditor. In short, an internal auditor may increase the effectiveness of an entity's control environment and can assume an important role as an in-house advisory function that offers analysis and assurance to the board as to the functioning of the risk management and internal control systems.

The internal audit function has become a major support function for management, the audit committee, the board of directors, the external auditors, and other key stakeholders and it can play a key role in promoting and supporting effective organizational governance. However, tensions might exist because the internal audit team is asked to serve two masters: the management, and the board (or the board's audit committee). Management wants the internal auditor to provide both assurance and consulting based on broad operational skills that address risks, evaluate the efficiency of operations, and stimulate organizational action. On the other hand, the board (and its audit committee) is more interested in assurance regarding controls.

Internal auditing practitioners are increasingly being challenged to apply their expertise in much broader ways than ever before, such as evaluating emerging technologies, detecting and deterring fraud, analyzing the effectiveness of policies and procedures, and identifying opportunities to save the company and its shareholders money (U.S., The Institute of Internal Auditors).

1. RELATED RESEARCH

Empirical evidence regarding the effectiveness of internal control practices is very scarce. One reason is that data on internal control practices is not publicly available. In the literature, internal auditing related variables have often been used as proxies for internal control.

If external auditors use work produced by the internal audit to deliver the external financial statement audit, a concomitant reduction in the external-audit fee is expected to occur. Felix *et al.* (1998) suggest that lowering the external-audit costs is not just a by-product; rather, it is the primary reason why external auditors rely on internal-audit. There has been some research on how much of the savings, if any, are passed on to the customer. Wallace (1984) studies the relationship between audit fees and total expenditure on the internal-auditing department and finds that for every additional dollar invested in the internal-audit department, an average reduction in external-audit fees of 0.45$ is expected. Also Felix *et al.* (2001) analyze the extent to which internal-audit contribution affects the external-audit fee; they find that the greater the contribution made by the internal audit, the lower the external-audit fee. Specifically, if an audit client were to increase the contribution made by the internal audit to the financial-statement audit from no contribution to the mean level found in their sample (i.e., 26.57% of the financial-statement audit), the audit fee would decrease by approximately 18 percent. Moreover, they suggest that clients can affect the extent of internal-audit contribution by investing in internal-audit quality and by either managing internal-audit availability or facilitating greater coordination between internal and external audit. The greater the internal-audit availability, defined as the time internal auditors have available during the period of the financial-statement audit, the greater their potential contribution. Coordination efforts can involve assigning specific audit work throughout the audit year to the internal audit and managing internal-audit availability at year-end. Through the minimization of duplicate audit efforts, the effectiveness of the internal auditors' contribution to the financial-statement audit increases, and overall efficiency can be maximized.

SAS # 65 (AICPA) indicates that the quality (i.e., objectivity, competence, work performance) of the internal-audit function and the risk of material misstatement in the financial statements should be considered by external auditors in determining the contribution of the internal audit to the financial-statement audit. Studies by Maletta and Kida (1993), Maletta (1993), and Felix *et al.* (2001) indicate that as inherent risk[6] increases, certain internal-audit factors will increase in importance. In lower-risk conditions, simple factors such as the general availability of the internal auditors may be significant in determining the internal-audit contribution. However, in higher-risk conditions, more complex factors such as internal-audit quality and the extent of internal/external-audit coordination may emerge as the primary factors that influence the internal-audit contribution. That is, when inherent risk is higher, general availability is expected to be less important in determining the level of internal-audit contribution, while more complex factors, such as overall internal quality and the level of internal/external-audit coordination, should have a significantly greater effect on external auditors' reliance decisions. In line with this, Felix *et al.* (2001) find that as inherent risk increases, the effect of internal-audit availability on contribution diminishes, while the effect of coordination on contribution increases.

Evidence on the effectiveness of the internal audit function in Belgian companies is as scarce as abroad. A recent study by Willekens, Bruynseels and Heiremans (2005) reports for a sample of listed Belgian companies a clear positive association between the presence of an internal-audit function and transparency about financial risk management practices. However, no unambiguous association is found with transparency about other risk management practices.

---

6 Inherent risk, broadly speaking, is the risk of a material misstatement in the unaudited information assuming the absence of internal-control procedures.

2. ACTUAL PRACTICE IN BELGIUM

In our 2003 sample, an internal audit function was present in 58 percent of the companies. The size of the internal-audit group is highly right-skewed: the median number is unity, but the mean is 3.14 and the max is 24. Outsourcing occurred only in one case.

3. ROUND-TABLE DISCUSSION

Internal control v internal audit

Internal control and internal audit get often mixed up. Internal control is put in place to help manage the company, says one academic; it is embedded in business processes, built into the system, and is preventive by nature. The French call this *contrôle première degrée*, while internal audit is *contrôle seconde degrée*; it adds a layer of monitoring to see if the system works the way it was designed and if it still fits the objectives. Internal audit is in a sense indirect verification.

Internal control can play an important post-acquisition role, an executive adds. The successful establishment of a corporate culture of integrity can be achieved by having very detailed and precise reports drawn up by the internal-control unit. The internal control then works as an example of how the culture is expected to be.

What should an internal audit department do?

In academe's view, the internal audit is placed right between internal control and the external audit. When defined in a broad sense, internal auditing also includes elements of internal control, and in that sense of the term a company definitely needs internal auditing. But when defined in a more narrow sense, an internal audit is not always necessary.

One academic adds that the internal audit function has now bifurcated into two strands. The first function has to do with built-in controls, with key monitors that have to be in place to obtain accurate information. It is a technical task that is an absolute necessity in today's IT world. The second function that has gained considerably in scope and importance is risk management. This comprises both elements of internal audit and internal control. It goes way beyond financial risk management. For example, compliance management may be an issue in a proper business-risk evaluation.

The academic colleagues agree and assert that there is no doubt that the scope of the internal audit can be very wide: it can also cover operational matters, IT, or financial-statement support. In the case of General Electric, its internal audit department apparently uses KPMG methodology, and KPMG's external auditors follow this internal audit: this way, not only the internal audit was insourced, but also a lot of the external audit was being insourced.

Auditors note that in Belgium the external auditor is not allowed to perform the internal audits for a client, which is a strange situation and supposedly rests upon the confusion of internal audit with internal control. The internal audit is just an audit, and therefore it cannot replace the system of internal control. The cost of internal audits has made it attractive to outsource this function. So until the promulgation of the new law the external auditor was often asked to take care also of the internal audit.

Table 18: Mandatory internal-audit departments?

"All listed companies should set up an internal audit department."				
	Agree	Disagree	Depends	Blank
Board of directors	5/7	0/7	2/7	0/7
Executive Committee	11/14	2/14	0/14	1/14
Capital providers	9/9	0/9	0/9	0/9
External auditors	7/11	4/11	0/11	0/11
Academics	5/8	3/8	0/8	0/8

While all academics clearly agree that the internal audit definitely has a use, they feel less comfortable with the statement that all firms should have one. Whether a company needs an internal audit department depends on how the firm is organized. The decision to set up an internal-audit department should be a regular economic allocation decision. Executives concur that, in itself, the system of internal audits provides no guarantee for efficiency. Along with the audit plan, compliance is the most important condition for a successful internal audit. Auditors indicate that there definitely should be an internal audit – and preferably outsourced. Outsourcing makes sense because companies themselves do not have the same opportunities to build auditing expertise: in many cases the internal-audit team of even big companies has a mere three or four members. An alternative worth considering is a mix of outsourcing and in-house work. This usefully reconciles the accumulation of know-how internally with access to fresh ideas from outside.

Internal audit: potentially a good support for the audit committee and the board

To some academics, the demand for internal auditing seems to come from management, which wants information on how the organization can be improved. Often, management even sets up an internal audit against the recommendation of their external auditor, one professor adds. But Table 16 only weakly agrees with this statement: even among auditors there is a majority in favour of an internal audit.

To board members, internal and external auditing are complementary. One board member argues that it is important that the CEO takes the responsibility in determining the extent and depth of the internal audit, as he bears the final responsibility for the figures delivered to the board. Also auditors stress the complementary nature of internal and external audits. The internal auditor can address a wider range of risks than the external auditor, says one auditor. An internal-audit function can be very interesting because it helps the audit committee or the board members – epecially the independent ones – to get an insight in the way the firm handles internal controls. Whereas the external auditor will primarily focus on the financial aspects, the internal audit can also look at, say, processes that affect client satisfaction. Thus, far from being redundant, the internal audit can add substantial value. It has to be recognized, however, that the quality of internal audits is not yet always what it should be.

Academics posit that it is important to see whom the internal audit reports to in order to evaluate properly the functioning of the internal audit. Internal-audit departments of two companies may perform totally differently. This was clear in the Enron case, where all the right governance structures where in place – on paper – but where in reality the governance mechanisms performed very poorly.

After this brief chapter on internal audits, we now address the fourth instrument that could strengthen investor trust in the corporate world: the external auditor.

4. CONCLUSIONS

Research related to internal auditing has mainly focused on its impact on external-audit fees. The empirical results show consistent evidence that increased levels of internal auditing can lower audit fees substantially.

The topics discussed during the round-table sessions are very much related to the usefulness of internal auditing. Most participants agree that the internal audit definitely has its use, but they do not think that all firms should be required to have one. Note, however, that recent Best-Practice codes on corporate governance very clearly require that companies set up an internal audit function. In the US, the installation of an internal audit function is mandatory. Note that in Belgium about 60 percent of listed industrial companies had an internal audit function in 2003.

REFERENCES

American Institute of Certified Public Accountants (AICPA). 2001. *Statements on Auditing Standards*. New York: AICPA.

Carey, P., R. Simnett and G. Tanewski. 2001. Voluntary Demand or Internal and External Auditing by Family Businesses. *Auditing: A Journal of Practice and Theory*, 19 (supplement).

DeZoort, F. T. and A. T. Lord. 1997. A review and synthesis of pressures effects in accounting. *Journal of Accounting Literature* 16: 28-85.

Felix, W.L., Jr., A.A. Gramling, and M.J. Maletta. 1998. *Coordinating total audit coverage: The relationship between internal and external auditors*. Altamonte Springs, FL: The Institute of Internal Auditors.

Felix, W.L., Jr., A.A. Gramling, and M.J. Maletta. 2001. The contribution of internal audit as a determinant of external audit fees and factors influencing this contribution. *Journal of Accounting Research* 39 (3): 513-534.

Felix, W.L., Jr., A.A. Gramling, and M.J. Maletta. 2003. *The Influence of Non-audit Service Revenues and Client Pressure on External Auditors' Decisions to Rely on Internal Audit*. Working Paper.

Maletta, M. J. 1993. An examination of auditors' decisions to use internal auditors as assistants: The effect of inherent risk. *Contemporary Accounting Research* (Spring): 508-525.

Maletta, M.J. and T. Kida. 1993. The effect of risk factors on auditors' configural information processing. *The Accounting Review* (July): 681-691.

Wallace, W.A. 1984.Internal auditors can cut outside CPA costs. *Harvard Business Review* (March-April): 16-20.

Willekens, M., Bruynseels, L. and A. Heiremans. 2005. Corporate governance en risicomanagement in België: Wat er was vóór Lippens. *Accountancy & Bedrijfskunde*. Maart 2005.

CHAPTER 4
THE EXTERNAL AUDIT

External-audit services are demanded as monitoring devices that reduce information asymmetries and agency costs between the company's managers and stakeholders by allowing a third (outside) party to verify the validity of financial statements. More specifically, one of the purposes of the external-audit function is to assure the timeliness and accuracy of the reporting of relevant information to shareholders. This assurance is needed because users of financial statements do not have the opportunity or time to verify whether the statements actually reflect underlying business transactions. Wallace (1980), for instance, points out that audits are demanded at least partly because they reduce noise and bias in financial reporting.

Generally speaking, external and internal auditors use similar documentation methods and share a general customer focus. Key differences in the two professions stem from the basic reason for obtaining the services. For external auditors, the demand for certification of financial information originates from the outside shareholders or from an external regulator. In contrast, the internal auditors are driven by the desire of management to monitor the internal processes that should ensure accuracy, efficiency, and effectiveness of operations (the Institute of Internal Auditors).

The actual usefulness of an external audit depends on the audit quality provided. According to DeAngelo (1981) the quality of the audit is defined as the joint probability that a given auditor will, firstly, discover a breach in the client's accounting system and, secondly, also report the breach. The probability that a given auditor will discover a breach in turn depends on the auditor's technical and technological capabilities, the audit procedures employed on a given audit, the extent of sampling, etc. The conditional probability of reporting a discovered breach depends on the auditor's independence from a given client.

1. RELATED RESEARCH

As auditing is mandatory (for certain types of companies), it is difficult to measure the impact external auditing has on financial reporting quality. One category of auditing studies has focused on assessing the impact of differential audit quality on financial reporting features (such as, for example earnings management). Another group of auditing studies has investigated whether big N audit firms exhibit differential audit reporting characteristics as compared to non-big N firms. There are also studies that looked at the determinants of audit pricing and investigate, amongst other things, whether quality differences lead to price differences. Finally, have there been studies that have assessed the impact of the joint supply of management advisory services and auditing on auditor independence.

a. AUDIT QUALITY: A MATTER OF SIZE?

Extant accounting studies provide strong support for the view that large audit firms supply higher-quality audits compared to small audit firms. DeAngelo (1981) argues that large audit firms have stronger incentives to protect their valuable reputations because they lose more clients (and hence more rents) if they supply low-quality audits. Similarly, Dye (1993) argues that large audit firms have more wealth at risk from litigation, and so large audit firms have stronger incentives to avoid litigation by supplying high audit quality. An alternative explanation is that larger auditors are more competent at obtaining or interpreting audit evidence (Hogan and Jeter, 1999). For example, large audit firms may have more staff with client – or sector-specific knowledge, or they may be more experienced in auditing large, complex companies.

The empirical evidence is (generally) consistent with large audit firms supplying higher-quality audits compared to small audit firms. For example, Mutchler *et al.* (1997) and Gaeremynck and Willekens (2003) find that Big-N audit firms issue more qualifications than non-Big-N audit firms, ceteris paribus. Teoh and Wong (1993) find that the relation between earnings announcements and stock-price reaction is stronger for companies audited by large audit firms, which suggests that investors perceive these companies' financial statements as more credible. Lennox (1999) observes that large audit firms' going-concern opinions are more accurate predictors of bankruptcy compared to small audit firms' going-concern opinions. He argues that large auditors are significantly more likely to give going-concern qualifications to failing companies and clean opinions to non-failing companies, because in their market segment it is easier to predict bankruptcy than for clients of small auditors.

b. EARNINGS MANAGEMENT

For most firms, management compensation is explicitly or implicitly a function of some earnings-based performance measure. This emphasis on earnings encourages managers to meet earnings targets. The effectiveness of auditing, and its ability to constrain the management of earnings, is expected to vary with the quality of the auditor. High-quality auditors are less willing to accept questionable accounting methods and are more likely to detect and report errors and irregularities. The most common proxy that has been used for audit quality is a dummy variable Big-N/non-Big-N, where Big-N auditors are deemed to be, by and large, the higher-quality auditors.

Consistently with this view, Francis *et al.* (1999) find that Big-N audit firms constrain earnings management more than non-big-N audit firms. Similarly, DeFond and Jiambalvo (1991,1993) report that, excluding fraudulent firms, the incidence of accounting errors is negatively associated with the presence of Big-N auditors. They also find that audit conflicts over income-increasing accounting choices are positively associated with the presence of Big-N auditors. For Belgium, VanderBauwhede *et al.* (2003) find that for the large-client market segment, big-N firms do constrain income-decreasing earnings management more than non-Big-N audit firms. However, in the small non-listed client segment of the market, no differences are found between big-N and other firms.

c. AUDITOR REPORTING

Auditor-reporting studies have examined the relationship between audit-report type and firms' financial distress. Two distinct tracks were followed. Some studies (see, for example, Mutchler 1985, Dopuch et al. 1987, Menon and Schwartz 1987, Bell and Tabor 1991, Chen and Church 1992, Mutchler et al. 1997, Gaeremynck and Willekens 2003) investigate financial and other determinants of the auditor's choice of report type, especially determinants of going-concern qualifications. Others (see, for example, Hopwood et al. 1989, Citron and Taffler 1992, Vanstraelen 2002, Gaeremynck and Willekens 2003) examine the impact of audit-report type on the probability of future bankruptcy and/or firm survival (the self-fulfilling prophecy hypothesis).

The impact of financial condition on audit-report type is widely documented (for example, Mutchler, 1985; Dopuch et al. 1987, Bell and Tabor, 1991; Chen and Church, 1992). In all these studies it has been shown that the receipt of a non-clean opinion is determined by weak financial performance (signalled by liquidity, solvency and profitability problems). Another interesting related question is whether big N auditors exhibit differential audit-reporting behaviour as compared to non-big N auditors, or in other words, whether there is evidence of product differentiation (as to reporting) in the Belgian audit market. In the US, Mutchler et al. (1997) found evidence that the audit-report type is influenced by the size of the audit firm. Gaeremynck and Willekens (2003) report some evidence supportive of product differentiation between Big N and non-big 6 auditors in the Belgian audit market, as they find reporting differences between these two types of audit firms. Note however, that these are only found for the sub-sample of firms that voluntarily liquidate, that is where financial difficulties are less pronounced. When a firm's financial problems are more explicit, and subsequent bankruptcy is highly probable, they find no audit-reporting differences between big N and non-big N firms. The latter 'non-result' is also found by Vanstraelen (2002).

The evidence regarding the impact of audit-report type on business termination is scarce and results are mixed (Citron and Taffler, 1992; Hopwood et al., 1987). Citron and Taffler (1992), who use a univariate analysis, do not find evidence for the self-fulfilling prophecy hypothesis. In contrast, the multivariate results of Hopwood et al. (1989) show that consistency qualifications as well as going-concern opinions are significant in explaining bankruptcy the year before failure. More recently, Gaeremynck and Willekens (2003) provide evidence on the endogenous relationship between audit-report type and business termination. Controlling for the endogenous relation between audit-report type and business termination, their findings provide support for the self-fulfilling prophecy stating that financial difficulties become even more severe after receiving a non-clean audit opinion.

d. AUDIT PRICING

Based on the empirical evidence of high supplier concentration in the audit market, early audit fee research was mainly inspired by concerns about price competition in the audit market. In his seminal paper, Simunic (1980) proposed a model of audit pricing to test for competition in the US audit industry. He *assumed* that price competition prevails in the small auditee market segment because of the lower supplier concentration in this segment, but that the large auditee market may not be competitive because of big N (then big 8) concentration. By comparing pricing in the two market segments, Simunic draws conclusions about competition in the audit market. From the results of his study the hypothesis that the audit market is competitive could not be rejected, as no significant premia were found for big N (then big 8) firms in the large client segment of the market. Many subsequent studies adopted a similar approach to study audit pricing (see, for example, Francis, 1984; Palmrose, 1986a and 1986b; Francis and Simon, 1987; Ettredge and Greenberg, 1990; Pong and Whittington, 1994; Lee, 1996 and DeFond et al., 2000). Unlike Simunic, most studies report a significant big N audit fee premium and explain this finding by product differentiation by the big N and not as a result of big N market power. The different findings as to big N premia are explained by size differences in the client samples under investigation.

Later audit fee studies (see, for example, Pearson et al., 1994; Craswell et al., 1995; Deis et al., 1996; and DeFond et al., 2000) were mainly concerned with specific determinants of audit fees, such as the effect of auditor switching, auditor concentration and auditor industry specialization.

Fees studies have also been done outside the U.S. For example, Francis (1984), Francis and Stokes (1986), Craswell et al. (1995) report evidence on the *Australian* market; Chan et al. (1993), Pong and Whittington (1994), Taffler and Ramalinggam (1982) on the *UK* market; Firth (1985) on the *New Zealand* market; Anderson and Zeghal (1994) on the *Canadian* market; and Chung and Lindsay (1988), Dominica Suk-yee Lee (1996), Gul (1999) and DeFond et al. (2000) on the *Hong Kong* market; Willekens and Achmadi (2003) for the *Belgian* audit market. Overall, we can conclude that: 1) a fairly robust audit fee model seems to explain 50%-70% of audit fee variations across the world, including auditee size, client complexity and riskiness as explanatory variables, and 2) significant price premia for big N firms are observed worldwide. Note that almost all prior audit fee studies used samples of public clients.

In a recent study, Menon and Williams (2001) report evidence on long-term trends in audit fees in the US audit market. They find that fees increased in the 1980s but stayed flat in the 1990s. In particular, a significant increase in fees is noted in 1988, which the authors attribute to an expansion of audit effort as a response to the issuance of the expectations gap standards. The evidence also indicates a short-term but not a long-term effect of the big 8 mergers in 1989 on audit pricing. Some changes in the audit fee model over the sample period (1980-1997) are also documented. For example, the magnitude of the coefficients for accounts receivable and inventory have declined which can be attributed to audit productivity improvements. Important to note is that the sample in the study was restricted to clients of big 6 firms that voluntarily disclosed audit fees in the period 1980-1997. This implies that no evidence is obtained on the non-big 6 client segment of the market, nor on the privately held firm segment of the audit market.

Note that Hay, Knechel and Wong (2005) provide a meta-analysis of audit fee determinants across 88 audit fee studies. The audit fee is determined by a wide range of variables. On the one hand, client-firm characteristics have a serious impact on the time invested and the risk faced by the auditor. On the other hand, also audit-firm characteristics have an impact on the audit fees. The audit-pricing literature suggests that for clients with certain characteristics, an auditing firm may either charge a price premium to cover its potential litigation risk, or exert extra effort to produce a more defensible audit. Five client characteristic are considered to have a possible impact on the audit price: firm size, the ownership type, organizational complexity, the financial situation, and board characteristics. Certain auditor-firm characteristics may have an influence on the audit fee. The two characteristics that are generally considered are economies of scale and product differentiation or specialisation.

Two studies have been done on audit pricing in Belgium. Willekens and Achmadi (2003) provide evidence on audit pricing in the private client segment of the audit market in 1989 and 1997. They investigate whether (1) audit pricing is competitive in the private client segment of the audit market, and (2) the increase in market concentration between 1989 and 1997 resulted in more or less price competition. They report that audit fees are significantly associated with the incumbent auditor's market share both in 1989 and 1997. This result is similar to prior studies on pricing in the public client segment of the market. It is not clear whether this finding implies that there is a lack of competition in the market or whether the price premium is due to product differentiation. Willekens and Achmadi (2003) also report some interesting results regarding the change in the pricing model between 1989 and 1997. The evidence strongly suggests that price competition increased between 1989 and 1997.

Knechel and Willekens (2004) investigate audit pricing in the public client segment of the Belgian audit market and find that internal control, risk management and governance significantly affect audit demand and pricing. In particular, audit fees (and hence audit demand) are higher when a company has an audit committee, discloses a relatively high level of financial risk management and has a larger percentage of independent board members. Audit fees are lower when a company discloses a relatively high level of compliance risk management. The latter result indicates that controls are only complementary as long as they voluntary, as mandated controls act as substitutes for non-mandated controls.

e. NON-AUDIT SERVICES: ANATHEMA?

Independent auditing is an essential feature of a well-functioning capital market, and regulators have long been concerned with potential threats to auditor independence. Providing non-audit services may impair auditor independence because the fees from these services make auditors financially dependent on their clients, and because the nature of the services often put auditors in managerial roles. In addition, the provision of audit and non-audit services to the same firm may result in a serious conflict of interest, as the audit firm is serving two different sets of clients: the management when providing management consulting services and, in the case of the audit, the audit committee, the board, the shareholders and all those who rely on the audit report. The conflict of interest may result in lower audit quality and an decreased likelihood that the auditor will denounce earnings management attempts. An auditor concerned about the possible loss of non-audit fee revenue may be less likely to disagree with management's accounting choices, thus leaving their customers more leeway to manage earnings. As a result of these concerns, in many countries restrictions regarding the joint supply of audit and advisory services have been pronounced.

Predictably perhaps, auditors (and others) beg to disagree. They object that the provision of non-audit services improves audit quality and can thus reduce earnings management. Also, an auditor will think twice before giving up independence, it is argued. First, auditors may face significant legal sanctions from poor-quality audits. Second, reputational penalties constrain the behaviour of audit firms because the gains from acquiescing to any one client's demands are outweighed by the reputational losses that would be imposed by other clients who value the audit firm for its reputation for independence (DeAngelo, 1981). Along similar lines, Dopuch *et al.* (2001) demonstrate that the increase in reputational capital resulting from the provision of non-audit services will increase auditor independence and audit quality, *ceteris paribus*.

The empirical evidence on whether or not non-audit services actually impair independence is not fully conclusive. A recent study by Frankel *et al.* (2001) supports the independence concerns, finding that non-audit service fees are associated with clients that report larger magnitudes of discretionary accruals and are better at meeting earnings targets – two factors associated with earnings management. In contrast, DeFond *et al.* (2002) find no evidence that non-audit service fees impair auditor independence, at least when independence is measured by auditors' propensity to issue going-concern audit opinions. They further find that auditors are more likely to issue going-concern opinions to clients paying higher audit fees, implying that auditors seem to behave with relatively greater independence towards these clients. Reynolds and Francis (2001) obtain similar results. They find that relatively larger audit clients (for which the auditor is expected to have the greatest financial dependence) tend to report significantly lower discretionary accruals than do smaller clients. Nor do Reynolds and Francis (2001) find any evidence that auditors are more lenient in issuing going-concern reports to larger clients.

The relation between earnings management and non-audit fees is further explored by Gore *et al.* (2001), who report evidence that earnings management activities to avoid losses or drops in earnings are positively associated with the ratio of non-audit fees to total fees for non-Big-N auditors but not for Big-N auditors. The difference in the effectiveness of Big-N and non-Big-N auditors in constraining earnings management widens as the non-audit fee ratio increases. That is, when the provision of non-audit services is relatively high, smaller auditors seem to be less able to resist aggressive accounting by their clients, while big-N firms may be unaffected.

2. ACTUAL PRACTICE IN BELGIUM

The market share of the Big-N auditors among our listed companies is 81.2 percent in 2003, down from 90.2 in 2001 (probably following the demise of

Andersen).[7] In 18 annual reports, a supplier of management auxiliary services is identified, and in 15 cases out of these 18 the supplier was also the external auditor.

3. ROUND-TABLE DISCUSSION

Should auditors curtail all forms of earnings management and use formal analytical procedures and tools to identify "abnormal" accounting numbers and earnings?

All parties tend to agree that earnings management is reprehensible and should be actively looked for, as can be inferred from Table 19. One academic disagrees with the second part of the statement because the concept of "abnormal" does not have any objective meaning in practice. Especially formal models of what constitutes "normal" figures are useless: what academic models construe to be abnormal is mostly meaningless to practitioners. An auditor's opinion may be that the statements are of high quality even if the financial statement includes unusual accruals. When numbers look eccentric, the auditor probably saw this too and has already verified them more carefully.

Table 19: Auditors and earnings management

"Auditors should curtail earnings management and use formal analytical procedures to identify "abnormal" accounting numbers and earnings."				
	Agree	Disagree	Depends	Blank
Board of directors	6/7	1/7	0/7	0/7
Executive Committee	11/14	1/14	0/14	2/14
Capital providers	7/9	1/9	0/9	1/9
External auditors	9/11	2/11	0/11	0/11
Academics	7/8	1/8	0/8	0/8

Auditors state that they want to deliver an independent opinion, maintain a high reputation and respect auditing standards. True, the occasional exception cannot be ruled out. However, it is really difficult to prove to the public that these exceptions are really exceptions, because an auditor is not allowed to publicly speak about the adjustments that a company has made following an earlier intervention by the auditor.

[7] The tenure of the auditor may have been shrinking, between 2003 and 2001, but also this may be an Andersen effect again. Also, suspiciously many firms report a 3-year tenure (probably the length of a standard contract rather than the total tenure).

Is income smoothing part of earnings manipulation?

Some academics do not regard income smoothing as necessarily pejorative, because shareholders value predictability. The difference with true earnings manipulation is that in the case of smoothing the company only reshuffles the timing of recognition of income that is actually there. In the case of manipulation, in contrast, income is created artificially. However, it is often very difficult to discriminate between smoothing and manipulation. Income recognition remains one of the key elements in earnings management.

The crisis in public trust

A representative of the capital providers states that the current crisis of trust has little to do with the issue of audit fees versus consulting income. If manipulation and fraud happen, the reason is not that auditors have so much work that they do not notice the problems in the statements. Rather, the investor emphasizes, more often than not the real problem is that they did notice but they did not report it. The problem is not with the structure of the board, but with the failure of the audit committees and especially the failure of the external auditor. If an auditor has some questions, he should not wait for information to appear, but should look actively for answers.

A second source for the public-trust crisis, the investors' representative continues, is relations with the analyst. PR/IR officers should have provided correct information to the analysts, thus preventing the gaming that has taken place in the late nineties. Figures that were supposed to truly and fairly represent the situation of the firm were frivolously massaged to predict a glowing future, causing the stock prices to rise. Auditors sat by and watched, in complicit silence. It is important to keep in mind how external auditors are organized; once one does exactly that, it becomes clear that their commercial interests are more important than their duty to the general public.

Many executives tend to agree with the above and state that the external auditor should provide useful information and suggestions to the firms and should indicate whether and when the value as presented in the books does not reflect the real value. One executive wonders why the board hires an external agent for the audit if the board itself remains fully responsible for the figures anyway.

One of the academics has a totally different perspective on the causes of the current crisis. The problems with Enron, Quest, Global Crossing and WorldCom were only systemic in the way that they used a method developed by Andersen to trade network capacity, which allowed to record enormous amounts of money as revenue. One of the major problems of auditors – and this was certainly the case with Deloitte & Touche in the Ahold case – is that they cannot go to the press when they have found a problem. The auditor basically has to sit still until the case explodes in their hands.

Other participants from the financier side state that part of the accounting problem in the U.S. is related to the board seeking coverage against litigation. For example, in the U.S. GAAP tradition, people are covered from the moment that certain formal rules are followed. It is a system of box-ticking. Anything listed in the GAAP manuals is allowed even if makes no sense in the case at hand. In this way, there is a certain loss of ethical awareness. The discussants go on stating that this problem is less prominent in the European system, where judgement and ethical awareness are still important. It is however clear that when the top of the firm acts on the basis of box-ticking, this practise will spread throughout the firm. An ethically strong business culture should be set at the top levels and pushed to all levels.

Another capital provider views investment bankers as a source of great damage to public trust: they promoted wrong valuation models and were the engine for dubious expansion strategies. But most of our discussants do not agree here. There is nothing inherently wrong with being enthusiastic about a business model. If people think it is important to look at essentially one criterion, that is their responsibility; from the bank's or firm's side there is no problem, as long as the information is correct. The reliability of the information presented is key, not the use to which it is put by others.

Cross-subsidization between auditors and consultants?

Table 20: Non-audit services by audit firms

"The provision of non-audit services lessens the auditor's independence and results in higher earnings manipulation."				
	Agree	**Disagree**	**Depends**	**Blank**
Board of directors	3/7	2/7	2/7	0/7
Executive Committee	7/14	1/14	1/14	5/14
Capital providers	7/9	1/9	0/9	1/9
External auditors	1/11	10/11	0/11	0/11
Academics	3/8	5/8	0/8	0/8

As to the admissibility of non-audit contracts, executives and investors are weary, while academics and board members tend to be much divided; but auditors want no restrictions (Table 20). Several academics stress that the public overestimates the links between the audit experts and the non-audit experts within one firm. In reality there is obviously some referral, and maybe some of the fees are split between the partners – but less so than is commonly assumed. They further point out that in the audit market, the customer is the shareholder and in the non-audit service market the customer is management. While maybe too much effort has been spent on servicing management, it remains far from clear whether this lack of balance really drives audit decisions: there are a lot of other factors influencing these. For example in the case of Enron the income balance between the two kinds of services was about 25 million USD versus 27 million USD. Maybe the true problem with Enron was that, to Andersen, this client was so important that the individual audit partner became too lax: to the accountants, losing the account probably looked worse than losing the non-audit business. There are also strong interpersonal dynamics between auditor and management, which often have an impact on the audit decision. Board members argue that in this issue, self-regulation is the only regulation that really works. Big auditors just followed the demand of the market.

If there is little threat from management advisory services, is there an advantage to knowledge spillovers?

One argument that is often used against the separation of audit and non-audit services, is that the audit firm would lose their best people if they cannot do anything but audits. Auditors add that the knowledge spillover of general consulting is usually not significant, but with other services – say, tax advice – there may be much more synergy. It is hard to do an audit without having a broad expertise on, for example, taxes or social security.

There should be in-depth specialization in an audit firm, a financier admits, but different services should nevertheless not be sold to the same client firm, because then one risks ending in a situation of self-audit. One of the obvious dangers is that the accounting firms' interests become too much aligned with those of management. As a consequence this may have an impact on the quality of the financial statements.

Has the role of the external auditor changed since the public-trust crisis? Has it grown?

Auditors think that the role of the auditor has not changed much following the crisis of trust. There now is a debate as to whether the auditor should only deliver attestation, or should also provide a judgement about internal control. But the profession's main task remains to deliver honest and objective opinions about financial statements. What the crisis *has* highlighted is the existence of the expectations gap surrounding the profession: the public really expects a guarantee from the auditor that the auditee company will not fail any time soon. However, the audit profession has never delivered this guarantee in the past, and will never be able to do so in future either.

Most academics agree that nothing really has changed, except perhaps that nowadays, when an auditor delivers a qualified report to a listed company, the auditor explains to the press why the audit qualification was given. The number of qualifications remains quite low; also, the few qualifications in the final report are often about problems with real-data verification rather than cases were management refused to revise the accounting decisions.

One academic objects that the size of fraud in the last four to five years has increased immensely. However, some other colleagues do not agree. Not even the size is unusual this time, they think: the direct economic impact of Enron's implosion, for example, was not that high. The whole case has been exaggerated and the main impact has been bad publicity. A third colleague objects that this ignores a huge collateral damage, the value destroyed on the stock market as a whole.

Audit fees currently do not reflect risk. Should they in future?

Table 21: Risk premia in audit fees

"Since audit fees do not contain risk premia, there should be a revision of audit fees and they should include risk premia."				
	Agree	**Disagree**	**Depends**	**Blank**
Board of directors	2/7	4/7	0/7	1/7
Executive Committee	1/14	10/14	0/14	3/14
Capital providers	2/9	7/9	0/9	0/9
External auditors	8/11	3/11	0/11	0/11
Academics	3/8	4/8	0/8	1/8

Most parties disagree that, as of now, riskier firms should pay more for their external audits, as can be appreciated from Table 21; only external auditors really believe the audit fees should be revised. A board member admits that, in principle, compensation should be related to the risk borne, but the external auditor does not run a greater risk than do other parties. Other board members add that the work done by the external auditor is not always of excellent quality in the first place, so that asking more money will not make auditors more popular.

One professor protests. Research indicates that the risk of the firm is not taken into account in determining the audit fee, she argues. No significant association has been detected between risk factors of the firm (like chance of failure or chance of fraud) and the level of the fee. If auditors are not paid to take more risk, they will refuse to audit the higher-risk clients. One board member replies that the statutory audit traditionally might have been the loss leader used to gain access to a firm's non-audit business, thus cutting the link between price and risk. But now that consulting is separated from the audit services, audit firms will raise their prices because the profitability of the audit services will be too low. Thus, in the future the link between risk and the level of the fee may very well emerge after all.

Auditors, in contrast, explain the current low levels of fees as the result of competitive market forces. After Enron and other crises, audit fees should go up, because of the series of new tasks that are demanded from the auditor. But not surprisingly, if auditors raise their fees, they will always risk the comment that they operate in an oligopolistic market without sufficient competitive pressure.

One academic concurs that Big-N auditors are often viewed as a collusive bunch of oligopolists. But research rejects this diagnosis and reveals lots of competition between the auditors; and competition lowers the price. A financier in our panel has doubts: how can competition wipe out an economically relevant cost? That is, should not every unrestricted and well-functioning market take into account the amount of risk, if that risk is really relevant? Another capital provider responds that auditors can and do diversify the risk, so that the net risk is lower than it appears to be at first blush. In addition, he argues, it is not correct to focus one's risk analysis on a single firm as it is too difficult to gauge an individual customer's risk and to estimate the probability of realisation of the risk. In short, it is quite logical to set fees taking into account only an average risk of a portfolio of firms.

What is the value of audit services? What is the marginal reduction in risk an auditor brings to the system?

Academics think that a company's internal system, installed by management, deals very well with a lot of routine operations, so there is very little risk here that the auditor can help reduce. In contrast, the auditor can play an especially positive role in non-routine operations and in situations where management has a biased view. The role of an audit is also one of a preventive nature, aimed at discouraging management from undertaking certain actions. It is clear that in some well-publicised cases the auditors did not perform their task effectively.

One of the investors in our panel argues that there is a growing structural problem in the organisation of Big-N auditors: the time spent by senior partners becomes relatively limited. As a substitute for the dwindling (but important) judgements by top people, clients get more working hours performed by less experienced staff. An auditor replies that the audit is an economic task and should be performed in a cost-effective way to keep the price acceptable. Moreover, the auditor is still bound to follow the same quality rules. Lastly, reviewing the quality of the auditor is one of the board's crucial tasks; any substandard delivery should trigger a demand for better quality.

Should the external audit go beyond financial-statement attestation?

Auditors respond positively to the above question: there certainly is a tendency to go beyond the financial statements and to look more at risks that might compromise the underlying objectives and processes that the organisation has in place. But auditing should still primarily be about financial statements.

What makes audit fees decline?

Academics point out that, although audit services have presumably a positive economic value, declining fees and plummeting incomes have been plaguing the industry for many years now. One common argument to explain the fee decline is that the quality of the audits has deteriorated and therefore audit fees have fallen. Others reverse the logic: the decline in the fees is at the root of the lower audit quality. Still other explanations include the fierce competition among auditors and the cross-subsidization between audit and non-audit services.

Restoring public trust by mandatory rotation?

A representative of the financing side argues that one way to restore public trust may be to impose a mandatory rotation of the auditing firm, say every three years. But some colleagues from academe are less than fully convinced and stress the disadvantages. Research, in fact, shows that more rotation is associated with a higher occurrence of audit failure. The chance of an audit failure is greatest when the auditor has been contracted very recently because the auditor needs some time to get to know the firm. Capital providers, who tend to be in favour of rotation, riposte that this may indeed be true for technical elements of the firm. But the consequences of a technical audit failure can not be compared to the consequences of an audit failure in the situation where auditor and CEO have already been working together for ten years, putting in danger the reputation of the entire audit profession.

One of the professors reminds us that, instead, the key to audit quality may be partner rotation within the same auditor firm, the Sarbanes-Oxley solution. Partner rotation is not so much a mechanism to prevent fraud; instead, it sustains the quality of the audit by bringing in "fresh eyes". But other academics raise many questions about the practical implementation of such a rotation system. Which partners should rotate? Is it rotation of the senior partner? Should it not also include members of the audit team, and how many?

Restoring public trust by ethical values?

Some of the executives recommend another approach to restore public trust. They emphasize that one of the main responsibilities of the board is to select the right people, not only on the basis of their professional qualifications, but certainly also for their ethical values. The crucial question is whether public trust is achieved via just general mechanisms or whether, in addition, the ethical values of each person should also be considered. They assert that value systems may be more effective to achieve public trust than corporate-governance mechanisms.

But the implementation of an effective value system still depends on the audit committee as well as the external and internal auditor. Along the same lines, one executive objects that greater public trust cannot be achieved by just hiring credible people: a lot of mechanisms have still to be put in place to be viewed as trustworthy, because the public strongly believes in regulation. This is especially true for the Anglo-Saxon world.

Restoring public trust by narrowing the expectations gap and accomplishing better understanding of the auditor's role?

Auditors take a totally different perspective: the auditor should try to narrow the expectations gap. This can be done by explaining the audit's role to the public. The expectations gap is all about the difference between what the public thinks the auditor should deliver and what he actually can deliver. Auditors further assert that they have an important preventive role – fraud prevention – but are not allowed to talk about their successes. So people do not know the role of the auditor. However, even if auditors could say all they'd like to say, the expectations gap would not completely disappear: the stakeholder really expects zero risk, and no auditor can deliver that. Auditing is not an exact science with foolproof test procedures.

Auditors do a poor job communicating what they are doing. They use their own risk-based systems and base their final judgement upon it, but they should better explain how this judgement was reached. Anyhow, better communication about the profession will not be easily attained, since there is generally no interest from the press in the auditor's story. What is also underestimated, according to auditors, is the value an auditor adds by safeguarding the quality of the financial statements. Often the rules are so complex that the financial managers and the CFO depend on the expertise of the auditor for qualitative financial statements. Again, this is an important part of the auditor's job that is not always fully understood.

Auditors argue that the recent strong rise in the directors' liability may serve to improve the playing field of the profession. In order to cover their own risks, board directors will not take responsibility without being sure about the audit quality. It should be possible to close the expectations gap at the board-*v*-auditor level even if it is impossible vis-a-vis the general public. Auditors have to convince audit committees and management about their side of the job and this will lead to more appropriate fees for audit services.

Another auditor suggests that the party to be cured of the expectations gap is not so much the public as the courts of law and the legislators. Indeed, one reason why it may be impossible to close the expectation gap, according to auditors, is the fact that auditors are known to have deep pockets. When a company goes bust, frequently the only party lawyers can turn to is the auditor. The blame is put there where the money is. In this way an image is created that the blame lies with the auditors. Putting a cap on the maximum liability an auditor can face would reduce the incentives to play that game.

Restoring public trust by requiring the audit partner's personal signature on the report?

Would things be better if the personal reputation of the audit partner were at stake by making him or her sign the audit report not in the name of the firm, but in his own name, as is the rule in Belgium? Some academics and capital providers do not think so. Such a rule ignores the influence that structures and systems may have on a person. The culture created within the firm is very important, and should always be taken into account when considering responsibilities. Why and how the culture or code of conduct was established should also be considered. Thus, in shifting responsibility to one person, one ignores the fact that there usually is a multi-layered problem – on the level of the individual, the structures within the firm, and the structures in the market. A capital provider agrees: it actually is a dangerous evolution to put full responsibility with the individual auditing partner. Manipulation often is inherent to the business model and culture promoted by the board or the management. The external auditor cannot take full responsibility when the firm's incentive plan indirectly stimulates people to manipulate figures. There is a joint responsibility.

An academic argues that the risk of individual blames are not required to motivate partners: the name of the audit firm is known and this is what counts, because this firm will suffer a decrease in reputation and other negative consequences from an audit scandal.

Restoring public trust by removing auditing from the commercial sphere?

In some instances like food quality preservation, the control function is not assigned to a private, commercial partner but to a government or quango. Some of the capital providers and auditors are not convinced that this is the way forward in the case of auditing. The interaction between auditor and firm is seen as being very important. Still, it is necessary that the auditor can credibly guarantee the validity of the figures, and to achieve this, a less drastic step may be required than de-privatisation: cutting the non-audit business away from the auditing firm.

Auditors object that they may not be possible to attract top-level people in all domains if the audit firm is only allowed to do the financial audit. The auditors should convince the public and the regulators that the best way to guarantee audit quality is to have strong audit firms. Capital providers, in contrast, fully agree that the consulting activities should be fully separated from the audit activities.

Restoring public trust via disclosure by the auditor (1): should audit firms disclose more information related to the quality they provide to clients?

Table 22: Disclosure of audit-quality information

"As audit quality has an impact on auditor reporting, audit firms should disclose more information related to the quality they provide to clients."				
	Agree	Disagree	Depends	Blank
Board of directors	3/7	2/7	0/7	2/7
Executive Committee	11/14	0/14	0/14	3/14
Capital providers	8/9	1/9	0/9	0/9
External auditors	4/11	4/11	0/11	3/11
Academics	6/8	1/8	0/8	1/8

In our survey, academics and auditors are divided as to the merits of providing more information on the effort behind the audit report; but all other parties are in favor. With respect to the above question, an executive opens the discussion with the statement that the opinion of the auditor contains a lot of information, although it is quite technical. Knowledge that certain rules of an auditing institute must be respected, already provides a certain degree of quality assurance. But the discussant also stresses that auditors should do more than just follow rules; the auditor should make a selection of what is important and what is not and should mention which issues are important for which stakeholders.

All the same, executives also believe that the role of the auditor should not be overstated; he is only one piece of the pie. An auditor evaluates the accounts of a firm in light of a number of external criteria. But a sufficiently determined management can almost surely fool the auditor. Auditors may detect certain things, but fundamentally, the integrity of the figures presented to the auditor is what is really important. It is a pipedream to believe the auditor in himself can resuscitate public trust.

One of the academics remarks that disclosing the quality of an audit to the public is not an easy task in the first place. And if defining and measuring the quality of an audit is already hard enough, comparisons across auditees and auditors become even more problematic. A colleague argues that, in Belgium, auditors do already provide information about the number of hours worked and the composition of the audit team to the institute of auditors (IBR). The IBR uses this info to verify that enough effort went into the audit. Would it not be useful, then, to publicly disclose this information? Others have their doubts: they are not sure that working hours are a good proxy for quality.

Still, additional information should be given, some auditors believe, taking into account the expectations of all stakeholders. One area where there is a lot of potential for clarification as part of the War on Expectation Gaps is internal controls. There appears to be a misconception about the role the auditor should play in this. Auditors should make clear that it is up to the company's management to install the system of internal control, and that once installed it is primarily the board that should evaluate the management's efforts. The external auditor really is only last in line with his certification that the internal control system seems to be appropriate for the company.

It is nevertheless amazing, a professor muses, how boilerplate the auditor's report is, considering all the money that goes into auditing. This seems like a huge mismatch. The discrepancy can be explained by three factors: firstly, plain laziness; secondly, the legal aspects (including the potential liabilities an auditor can face); and thirdly, confidentiality. There is a difference between what is been reported to the public and what is reported to the board and management. Therefore, the auditor's official report should be regarded as mainly a legal document, with the chief purpose to fulfil legal requirements and giving wide berth to any risk of damaging the customer's reputation. What the auditor confidentially reports to the board is a totally different story.

Restoring public trust via disclosure by the auditor (2): What could be disclosed?

Academics point out that because of the difficulty of measuring audit quality, it really comes down to how confident the auditor is that the financial statements are not misstated and can be relied on. The invisible nature of the product is not well understood. There are really no tools to measure it, and looking at the person.hours spent on the job does certainly not tell the whole story. To get a better idea of the quality, the only source of information may be the logbook of disciplinary actions undertaken by the Institute of Auditors.

One of the academics points out that the public seems to ask from the auditor to give information that will enable him/her to discriminate the audit quality on a case-by-case basis. With an invisible-quality product this is reduced to an issue of trust: either an auditor is considered to be trustworthy or he is not. So what auditors need to work at is increasing their credibility and reputation. Auditors are in a difficult position; every day they collectively perform thousands of audits and very rarely one of these goes wrong. But auditors cannot talk about all the times they have been doing a good job. Another reason why auditors get the blame when something happens is that they simply have deep pockets. So it is in the self-interest of the other parties to lay the blame there.

A representative of a large auditing firm highlights that, to help build confidence, Big-N auditors now communicate in their annual report about what they consider to be quality aspects of the profession: good ethical behaviour, integrity and competence. A lot of effort is also going into the code of conduct and training, two important means to obtain these key elements.

This discussion finishes our review of the four bodies that are commonly used used to reduce the agency problem between stakeholders and management: the board, the audit committee, and the internal and external auditors. In the two remaining chapters, we turn to the intended product of all these efforts – more information to the stakeholders. Specifically, we shall ask whether more information helps and how much information is actually provided in Belgium.

4. CONCLUSION

Empirical research about external-audit effectiveness has mainly focused on three fields of research: audit quality, audit pricing and the provision of non-audit services. It is often argued that large audit firms have greater wealth at risk and therefore have a bigger incentive to provide high quality services. Empirical, mainly US, evidence is consistent with this argument in finding that a) large audit firms constrain their clients' earnings-management practices more than do smaller firm; and b) provide more non-clean audit opinions, ceteris paribus.

A rich literature exists on the determinants of audit fees. Audit fees are determined by a wide range of variables. On the one hand, client-specific characteristics have an impact on amount of work and risk faced by the auditor. On the other hand, also audit-firm characteristics play a role. Empirical studies show a positive relationship between audit fees and size, public ownership and organizational complexity of the client-firm and product differentiation of the audit firm. In addition, audit fees are negatively associated with the financial Policy makers, amongst others often suggest that providing non-audit services may impair auditor independence.

The empirical evidence regarding auditor independence is mixed. Some studies confirm this concern, finding that non-audit fees are associated with higher levels of earnings management. However, other papers report a positive relationship between the provision of non-audit services and auditor independence.

The opinion of the round table participants was equally divided concerning this issue.

REFERENCES

Anderson, Teresa and Daniel Zeghal. 1994. "The pricing of audit services: Further Evidence from the Canadian Market." *Accounting and Business Research*, (Summer): 195-207

Bell, T. and R. Tabor. 1991. Empirical Analysis of Audit Uncertainty Qualifications. *Journal of Accounting Research* 29 (Autumn): 350-370.

Chan, Philip, Mahmoud Ezzamel and David Gwilliam. 1993. "Determinants of Audit Fees for Quoted UK Companies." *Journal of Business Finance and Accounting*, (November): 765-786

Chen, K. C.W., and B. K.Church. 1992. Default on debt obligations and the issuance of going concern opinions. *Auditing: A Journal of Practice and Theory* 11: 30-49.

Citron, D. B,. and R.J. Taffler. 1992. The audit report under going concern uncertainties: an empirical analysis. *Accounting and Business Research* 22: 337-345.

Craswell, A., J. Francis and S. Tayor. 1995. Auditor brand name reputations and industry specializations. *Journal of Accounting and Economics* 20: 297-312.

DeAngelo, L. 1981. Auditor size and audit quality, *Journal of Accounting and Economics* 3: 183-199.

DeFond, M.L. and J. Jiambalvo. 1991. Incidence and Circumstances of Accounting Errors. *The Accounting Review* 66 (3):643-655.

DeFond, M.L., and J. Jiambalvo. 1993. Factors related to auditor-client disagreements over income-increasing accounting methods. *Contemporary Accounting Research* 9: 411-431.

DeFond, Mark L., Jere R. Francis, and T.J. Wong. 2000. "Auditor Industry Specialization and Market Segmentation: Evidence From Hong Kong." *Auditing: A Journal of Practice & Theory*, (Spring): 49-66.

DeFond, M. L., K. Raghunandan, and K. R. Subramanyam. 2002. Do non-audit service fees impair auditor independence? Evidence from going concern audit opinions. *Journal of Accounting Research* 40 (4): 1247-1274.

Deis, Donald R. Jr. and Gary A. Giroux. 1996. "The Effect of Auditor Changes On Audit Fees, Audit Hours, and Audit Quality." *Journal of Accounting and Public Policy*, (Spring): 55-76

Dopuch, N., R, King, and R. Schwartz. 2001. *Auditors' independence: appearance vs. fact*. Working paper, Washington University.

Dye, R. 1993. Auditing standards, legal liability, and auditor wealth. *Journal of Political Economy* 101: 887-914.

Ettredge, Mike and Robert Greenberg. 1990. "Determinants of Fee Cutting On Initial Audit Engagements." *Journal of Accounting Research*, (Spring): 198-210

Firth, Michael. 1985. "An Analysis of Audit Fees and Their Determinants." *Auditing: A Journal of Practice & Theory*, (Spring): 23-37

Francis, J.R. 1984. The Effect of Audit Firm Size on Audit Prices – A Study of the Australian Market. *Journal of Accounting and Economics* 62:133-151.

Francis, Jere R. and Daniel T. Simon. 1987. "A Test of Audit Pricing in The Small-Client Segment of The US Audit Market." *The Accounting Review*, (January): 145-157

Francis, Jere R. and Donald J. Stokes. 1986. "Audit Prices, Product Differentiation and Scale Economies: Further Evidence From The Australian Market." *Journal of Accounting Research*, (Autumn): 383-393

Francis, J. R., E. L. Maydew, and H. C. Sparks. 1999. The role of Big 6 auditors in the credible reporting of accruals. *Auditing: A Journal of Practice & Theory* 18: 17-34.

Frankel, R., M. Johnson and K. Nelson. 2001. *Auditor independence and earnings quality*. Working paper, Michigan State University, Ann Arbor Michigan; MIT.

Gaeremynck, A. and M. Willekens. 2003. The Endogenous Relationship between Audit-Report Type and Business Termination: Evidence on Private Firms in a Non-Litigious Environment, *Accounting and Business Research*, Vol. 33-1: 65-79.

Gore, P., P. Pope and A. Singh. 2001. *Non-audit services, auditor independence, and earnings management*. Working paper, Lancaster University.

Gul, Ferdinand A.. 1999. "Audit Prices, Product Differentiation and Economic Equilibrium." *Auditing: A Journal of Practice & Theory*, (Spring): 90-100

Hogan, C. and D. Jeter. 1999. Industry specialization by auditors, *Auditing: A Journal of Practice and Theory* 18: 1-17.

Hopwood, W., McKeon, J., and J. Mutchler. 1989. A test of the incremental explanatory power of opinions qualified for consistency and uncertainty. *The Accounting Review* 34: 28-48.

Knechel, W. R. and M. Willekens. 2004. *The Role of Risk Management and Governance in Determining Audit Demand*. KULeuven Research Report no. 0463.34 pp.

Lee, Dominica S.. 1996. "Auditor Market Share, Product Differentiation and Audit Fees". *Accounting and Business Research*, (Autumn): 315-324

Lennox, C. 1999. Are large auditors more accurate than small auditors? *Accounting and Business Research* 29: 217-227.

Lennox, C. 2003. *Managerial Ownership and the Choice of Audit Firm*. Working Paper.

Menon, K., and K. B. Schwartz. 1987. An empirical investigation of audit qualification decisions in the presence of going concern uncertainties. *Contempory Accounting Research* 3: 302-315.

Mutchler, J. F. 1985. A multivariate analysis of the auditor's going- concern opinion decision. *Journal of Accounting Research* 23: 668-682.

Mutchler, J., W. Hopwood and J. McKeown. 1997. The influence of contrary information and mitigating factors in audit opinion decisions on bankrupt companies. *Journal of Accounting Research* 35: 295-310.

Palmrose, Zoe-Vonna. 1986. "Audit Fees and Auditor Size: Further Evidence". *Journal of Accounting Research*, (Spring): 405-411

Palmrose, Zoe-Vonna. 1986. "The Effect of Nonaudit Services on the Pricing of Audit Services: Further Evidence". *Journal of Accounting Research*, (Autumn): 405-411

Pearson, Tim and Grey Trompeter. 1994. "Competition in The Market for Audit Services: The Effect of Supplier Concentration On Audit Fees." *Contemporary Accounting Research*, (Summer): 115-135

Pong, Christopher K.M. and Geoffrey Whittington. 1994. "The Determinants of Audit Fees; Some Empirical Models." *Journal of Business Finance and Accounting*, (December): 1071-1095

Reynolds, J. K. and J. R. Francis. 2001. Does size matter? The influence of large clients on office-level auditor reporting decision. *Journal of Accounting and Economics* 30: 375-400.

Simunic, D. A. 1980. The pricing of audit services: Theory and evidence. *Journal of Accounting Research* 18 (Spring): 161-190.

Securities and Exchange Commission. 2000. *Final Rule: Revision of the Commission's Auditor Independence Requirements*. Washington D.C.

Taffler, R. J. and K. S. Ramalinggam. 1982. *The Determinants of Audit Fees in The UK: An Exploratory Studies*. Working Paper, City University Business School: London, England.

Teoh, S. H. and T.J. Wong. 1993. Perceived auditor quality and the earnings response coefficient. *The Accounting Review* 68: 346-66.

VanderBauwhede, H., M. Willekens and A. Gaeremynck. 2003. Audit Quality, Public Ownership and Firms' Discretionary Accruals Management. *The International Journal of Accounting*. Vol. 38-1: 1-22.

Vanstraelen, A. 2002. Auditor economic incentives and going-concern opinions in a limited litigious continental European business environment: empirical evidence from Belgium. *Accounting and Business Research*: 32-3: 171-186.

Wallace, W. A. 1980. *The Economic Role of the Audit in Free and Regulated Markets*. University of Rochester, reprinted in Auditing Monographs McMillan (1985).

Willekens, M. and C. Achmadi. 2003. Price Competition in the Audit Market: The Impact of Market Concentration and Market share on Audit Pricing. *The International Journal of Accounting*. Vol. 38-3: 431-456.

CHAPTER 5
TRANSPARENCY & DISCLOSURE

A critical challenge for any economy is the optimal allocation of savings to investment opportunities. While both savers and entrepreneurs would like to do business with each other, matching savings to business investment opportunities is complicated for at least two reasons. First, entrepreneurs typically have better information than savers about the true merits of investment opportunities. Second, entrepreneurs' communications with investors are not completely credible because investors know that entrepreneurs have an incentive to inflate the value of their ideas. These differences in information and conflicting incentives give rise to a "lemon" problem[8] that can potentially lead to a breakdown in the functioning of the capital market. For example, consider a situation where half the business ideas are "good" and the other half are "bad". If, *ex ante*, investors cannot distinguish between the two types of business ideas, entrepreneurs with bad ideas will try to claim that their ideas are good. Being aware of this effect, investors will value all ideas at a probability-weighted average level of the good and bad ones. Therefore, if the lemons problem is not fully resolved, the capital market will rationally tend to undervalue good ideas and overvalue bad ideas relative to the information available to entrepreneurs. The implication is that mostly bad projects will be presented to the capital market; the good projects will be withdrawn, and financed privately.

At the conceptual level there are several potential solutions to the lemons problem. A first avenue is through optimal contracts between entrepreneurs and investors, which are hoped to provide incentives for full disclosure of private information and thus eliminate the mis-valuation problem (Kreps, 1990). Another potential solution to the information asymmetry problem is regulation requiring managers to fully disclose their private information. In both cases, the issue is how to implement and enforce these solutions. Finally, the lemons problem can be reduced by effective information intermediaries, such as financial analysts and rating agencies, who engage in private information production to uncover managers' superior information.

---

8 "Lemon" is colloquial for a flawed car or another flawed product. In the absence of certification, quality assurance, warranties etc. delivered by credible intermediaries, uninformed buyers would be willing to pay only the probability-weighted average of the prices of good cars and lemons. This would not satisfy potential sellers of good cars, so that in the equilibrium only lemons are sold, at lemon prices.

Thus, the demand for financial reporting and disclosure arises from information asymmetry and agency conflicts between managers and outside investors, which impede the efficient allocation of resources in a capital-market economy. Disclosure and the institutions created to facilitate credible disclosure between managers and investors play an important role in mitigating these problems. However, perfect (unbiased) disclosure may not be optimal because of two reasons. First there may be a direct cost associated with producing and disseminating information. Second, since disclosure reveals information to competitors or others who interact strategically with the firm, it may make the firm lose competitive advantage or bargaining power in various contexts. This has important implications for the corporate-governance structure. If the disclosure policy allows some managerial filtering of information, it is up to the governance structure to force the manager to follow the optimal policy. It is therefore important to keep in mind that the disclosure policy is never independent of managerial incentives, information asymmetry and corporate governance.

Firms provide disclosure in three different ways: through mandatory disclosure, through voluntary disclosure and via intermediaries. Mandatory disclosure is provided through regulated financial reports, including the financial statements, footnotes, management discussion and analysis, and other regulatory filings. By creating minimum disclosure requirements, regulators reduce the information gap between informed and uninformed. In addition, some firms engage in voluntary communication, such as management forecasts, analysts presentations and conference calls, press releases, internet sites, and other corporate reports. Finally, there are disclosures about firms by information intermediaries, such as financial analysts, industry experts, and the financial press.

1. RELATED RESEARCH

Research on transparency focuses mainly on voluntary disclosure, and more specifically on the information role of financial reporting for capital markets.

a. FORCES FAVORING OR OPPOSING INCREASED DISCLOSURE

Disclosure studies assume that, relative to outside investors, managers have superior information on their firms' expected future performance. Researchers discuss six forces that affect managers' disclosure decisions: capital-market transactions, corporate-control contests, stock-linked compensation, litigation, proprietary costs and managerial-talent signalling. As some forces will push managers towards more disclosure and others towards less, the optimum is determined as a function of the quality of mandated disclosure and a trade-off of lower capital cost and litigation cost against higher proprietary and incentive costs.

The capital-market transactions hypothesis

Healy and Palepu (1993, 1995) hypothesize that investors' perceptions of a firm are important to corporate managers expecting to issue public debt or equity or to acquire another company in a stock transaction. Consequently, managers who anticipate such capital-market transactions have incentives to increase voluntary disclosure and reduce the information asymmetry problem, thereby reducing the firm's cost of external financing.

Barry and Brown (1985) and Merton (1987) hypothesize that investors demand a risk premium for bearing the adverse-selection risk[9] that arises when there is an information asymmetry between managers and outside investors. By reducing information risk through increased voluntary disclosure, managers seek to reduce their cost of capital. Several studies provide evidence on voluntary disclosure policies of firms issuing new capital. Lang and Lundholm (1993) document that analysts' ratings of disclosures are higher for firms issuing securities in the current or future periods. In a follow-up paper, Lang and Lundholm (1997) analyze disclosures specifically for firms that make equity offerings and find that there is a significant increase in disclosure beginning six months before the offering, particularly for the categories of disclosure over which firms have the most discretion.

The corporate-control contest hypothesis

The second hypothesis about corporate motivations for (non-)disclosure starts from the observation that boards of directors and investors hold managers accountable for current stock performance. In Chapter 1, on the board of directors, we mentioned that CEO turnover is associated with poor stock performance. The literature on voluntary disclosure hypothesizes that managers use corporate disclosures to reduce the likelihood of undervaluation or to justify poor earnings performance.

The core of the argument is that bad performance endangers the top managers' jobs. For example, Gilson (1989) reports a combined turnover rate for chairman, CEO, and president totalling 52% per year for firms that are in default, bankrupt, or restructuring debt and a turnover rate of still 19% per year for firms which are in distress but not showing public evidence of creditor negotiations. By contrast, Warner

9 The adverse selection mechanism is that well-informed parties refuse to trade at prices they know to be bad for them (and good for the counterpart), while being quite eager to trade at prices they know to be good for them (and bad for the counterpart). Thus, the badly informed agent tends to lose when playing against an insider.

et al. (1988) report turnover rates for these positions of only 11.5% per year in firms not experiencing any apparent financial difficulty. These employment concerns may lead managers of distressed firms to be more aggressive in predicting earnings than they otherwise would, in the hope that an overly optimistic forecast will delay their termination long enough for performance to improve and prevent their termination.

The stock-compensation hypothesis

Managers are usually rewarded in part by a variety of stock-based compensation plans such as stock-option grants and stock-appreciation rights. These types of compensation schemes provide incentives for mangers to engage in voluntary disclosures. Managers interested in trading their stock holdings have incentives to disclose private information to meet restrictions imposed by insider-trading rules. By doing so, they may also increase the liquidity of the firm's stock. Restrictions on insider trading further provide managers with incentives to make voluntary disclosures to correct any perceived undervaluation relative to their own information set prior to the expiration of stock-option awards.

Consistent with the hypothesis, Noe (1999) provides evidence that the incidence of management forecasts is positively associated with trading by insiders in the firm's stock. Aboody and Kasznik (2000) find that firms accelerate the release of bad news and delay disclosure of good news prior to stock-option award periods. Such a disclosure strategy ensures that decreases in the firm's stock price related to the arrival of bad news occur before, rather than after, the award date, while stock price increases related to the arrival of good news occur after, rather than before, the award. They hypothesize that CEOs opportunistically manage the timing of their information disclosures to increase the value of their awards. Finally, they suggest that the CEOs' incentives to manage investors' expectations around scheduled awards could be mitigated by setting award dates immediately after earnings announcements.

The litigation cost hypothesis

Litigation risk is a fourth factor that influences a firm's disclosure policy. The U.S. litigation environment imposes an asymmetric loss function upon firms, in the sense that a firm is more likely to be sued when there is a large stock-price drop at its earnings announcement (Kasznik and Lev, 1995). This loss function may encourage firms to forecast less optimistically or more pessimistically than they otherwise would have done in the absence of litigation. And erring on the downside is safe: Francis *et al.* (1994) find no shareholder lawsuits alleging pessimistic forward-looking information or omissions of favourable forward-looking information.

It is not *a priori* clear into what direction the threat of shareholder litigation affects managers' disclosure decisions. On the one hand, legal actions against managers for inadequate or untimely disclosures may encourage firms to increase voluntary disclosure. For example, Skinner (1994) hypothesizes that managers of firms with bad earnings news have an incentive to pre-disclose such information to reduce the cost of litigation. On the other hand, litigation may also reduce managers' incentives to provide disclosure, particularly of forward-looking information. This is likely to arise if managers believe that the legal system penalizes forecasts made in good faith because it cannot effectively distinguish between unexpected forecast errors due to chance and those due to deliberate management bias.

Empirical work by Skinner (1994, 1997) supports the incentive view rather than the disincentive one. In particular, Skinner finds that firms with bad earnings news are more than twice as likely to pre-disclose the poor earnings performance than are firms with good news. In addition, firms with negative earnings news are more likely to be subject to litigation. Finally, he demonstrates that although the probability of litigation is not reduced by voluntary earnings forecasts, settlement costs are reduced. Hence, he concludes that the expected costs of litigation are still reduced by more timely disclosure of bad news forecasts.

Francis *et al.* (1994) find that 62% of the firms in their litigation sample were sued over earnings forecasts or preemptive earnings disclosures. Thus, this is not a marginal issue. They compare this sample to a set of no-litigation firms that experienced comparable stock price declines, and find that 87% of that control sample had pre-announced an earnings decline. Thus, pre-announcing does seem to help avoid litigation. Looking for clues as to what factor succeeded in scaring these firms into pre-disclosing, Francis *et al.* notice that the average firm in their no-litigation sample is about ten times larger than in the litigation sample. Company size, they indicate, may be a significant determinant of litigation risk. One simple reason is that larger damages can be collected from larger firms. A second reason is the existence of a fixed cost to litigation: damages collected from suing too small a firm would not cover this fixed cost. Therefore, the probability of being sued is higher for a larger firm, and so are the potential damages. In light of this, the Francis *et al.* evidence is consistent with firms' optimally using disclosure to minimize litigation costs: larger firms expect to be sued more frequently and, therefore, choose to pre-disclose more often (Skinner, 1997).

However, the threat of litigation is less likely to deter managers from forecasting optimistically when it is more difficult to successfully sue them for issuing misleading forecasts. Rogers and Stocken (2003) find that managers that are more likely to face litigation, release less optimistic forecasts than managers less likely to face litigation, but this incentive is dampened indeed when it is more difficult to detect whether managers have misrepresented their forward-looking information. Further, when it is more difficult to detect forecast bias, they find that (*i*) managers are more likely to offer forecasts that increase their profits from insider transactions; and (*ii*) managers of financially distressed firms are more optimistic than those of healthy firms.

The managerial-talent signaling hypothesis

Trueman (1986) argues that talented managers have an incentive to make voluntary earnings forecasts to reveal their quality. A firm's market value is a function of investors' perceptions of its managers' ability to anticipate and respond to future changes in the firm's economic environment. The sooner investors infer that the manager has received information, the more favourable will be their assessment of the manager's ability to anticipate future changes and the higher will be the firm's market value.

The proprietary-cost hypothesis

Proprietary information allows firms to enjoy a competitive advantage and capture abnormal rents. Verrecchia (1983) and Darrough (1993) hypothesize that the firms' decisions to disclose information to investors is influenced by concerns that such disclosures can damage their competitive position in product markets. These studies conclude that firms can have an incentive not to disclose information that would weaken their competitive position, even if non-disclosure makes it more costly to raise additional equity. Obviously, the strength of this incentive appears to be sensitive to the nature of the competition, in particular whether firms face existing competitors or merely the threat of entry, and on whether firms compete primarily on the basis of price or long-run-capacity decisions.

Piotroski (1999) examines firms' decisions to provide additional market-segment disclosures. He concludes that firms with declining profitability and with less variability in profitability across industry segments are more likely to increase segment disclosures, consistent with the proprietary-cost hypothesis.

b. MEANS OF VOLUNTARY DISCLOSURE

Earnings forecasts

Prior studies have found that management earnings forecasts are perceived to convey credible firm-specific information, both for the analysts (Hassell *et al.* 1988, Baginski and Hassell 1990, Williams 1996) and stock-market participants (Ajinkya and Gift 1984; Waymire 1984; Jennings 1987; Han *et al.* 1989).

Adding balance-sheet information to earnings reports

Chen *et al.* (2001) argue that managers have incentives to voluntarily include balance-sheet information along with quarterly-earnings announcements when current earnings are relatively less informative, or when future earnings are relatively more uncertain. In these settings investors are likely to have a greater demand for additional value-relevant information to help assess the company's value. A logical management response to these demands is to disclose balance-sheet information if it is value-relevant information (Ohlson, 1995).

Balance-sheet information may to be helpful in interpreting the valuation implications of earnings when reported earnings differ from market expectations. Managers will feel motivated to explain to market participants why earnings diverge from expectations and what the valuation implications are of the divergence. Balance-sheet disclosures can serve for this purpose because such data can be useful in interpreting reported earnings (McGough and Podd, 1999). For example, working-capital accounts provide investors with relevant information about the nature of reported accruals.

Any instance where earnings are hard to forecast is a potential candidate for balance-sheet pre-disclosure. Firms in high-technology industries may be one example. These tend to make large investments in intangibles such as research and development, human capital, and brand-name development. They also operate in rapidly changing environments which make their future operations, and hence future earnings, relatively more uncertain. This may result in a greater demand for balance-sheet information. Investors are also likely to have a relatively greater demand for balance-sheet information when firms engage in merger and acquisition activity or when the company is young. Mergers and acquisitions are likely to have a substantial impact on firms' future operations, and hence increase the uncertainty related to their future earnings. Younger firms have greater uncertainty of earnings because their production activities and sales are likely to be less predictable. Stock-return volatility is a last aspect that is likely to be associated with balance-sheet disclosures. High stock-return volatility is consistent with greater uncertainty about future earnings, because the stock price is a function of expected future earnings.

Consistent with these expectations, Chen *et al.* (2001) find that managers voluntarily disclose balance sheets when current earnings are relatively less informative, or when future earnings are relatively more uncertain. Specifically, balance sheet disclosures are more likely in the following cases: (1) the industry is high-tech; (2) the firm reports a loss; (3) forecast errors are larger; (4) a merger or acquisition takes place; (5) the firm is younger; and (6) the company's stock returns are more volatile.

Conference calls

Increasingly often, corporate managers use conference calls to communicate with investors. Conference calls are often used to supplement other disclosures. For example, many conference calls now follow quarterly-earnings releases, and are used to provide analysts with more information about the release. A typical conference call includes a 15-20 minute presentation by management, followed by a 30-45 minute question-and-answer session. The company usually controls who is allowed to ask questions.

Conference calls are used in those situations and for those companies where a supplementation is beneficial. For example, if earnings contain large unusual or extraordinary items, conference calls can be used to explain the implications of these items to analysts. In addition, firms whose business operations are changing rapidly or are not well captured by the traditional financial reporting model may be more likely to use conference calls to help analysts assimilate earnings news. Consistent with this hypothesis, Frankel *et al.* (1997) find that firms in high-tech industries and with higher market-to-book ratios are more likely to use conference calls. Furthermore, they find that firms holding conference calls tend to be larger, are more profitable, go to the capital market more often, and are growing more rapidly than other firms – characteristics that also describe firms with better-than-average disclosure policies in general.

From the company's perspective, conference calls provide at least two benefits. First, the calls save time because management can talk to hundreds of analysts and money managers simultaneously. Second, every participant is provided with the same information at the same time, mitigating selective-disclosure problems.

Lastly, there are good reasons to expect that conference calls do provide information to call participants. The very fact that analysts and institutional investors do participate in conference calls already indicates that these calls probably provide specific information that is not contained in the original press release. Frankel *et al.* (1997) documents that this is true.

c. ECONOMIC GAINS FROM VOLUNTARY DISCLOSURE

A number of studies examine the economic consequences of voluntary disclosure. These studies argue that there are potentially three types of capital-market effects for firms that make extensive voluntary disclosures: improved liquidity for their stock in the capital market, a reduction in their cost of capital, and increased following by financial analysts.

Improved Stock Liquidity (lower bid-ask spread)

Diamond and Verrecchia (1991), and Kim and Verrecchia (1994) argue that voluntary disclosure reduces information asymmetries among informed and uninformed investors. As a result, for firms with high levels of disclosure, investors can be relatively confident that stock transactions occur at fair prices, increasing liquidity in the firm's stock. Consistently with this logic, Welker (1995) documents a significant negative relation between bid-ask spreads and the quality of the firm's disclosure as measured by analysts' ratings on disclosure.

In line with the findings of Welker (1995) and Healy *et al.* (1999), also Leuz and Verrecchia (2000) show that bid-ask spreads on the Neuer Market, which has higher disclosure requirements, are smaller than on the Frankfurt Exchange.

Reduced Cost of Capital and Cost of Debt

The adverse-selection fear, among investors, of losses from trading against better-informed agents translates into a lower stock price, that is, a higher discount rate for expected future earnings. In general, disclosure of information or elimination of uncertainties allows firms to reduce information asymmetries, thereby lowering their cost of equity capital. Botosan (1997) and Botosan and Plumlee (2002) provide a direct link by showing a negative relation between disclosure and the cost of equity capital for firms followed by few analysts and for firms in general, respectively. But contrary to expectations, in Canadian markets Richardson and Welker (2001) find a significant positive relationship between social disclosure and the cost of equity capital. The cost of equity penalty for firms with extensive social disclosure is however mitigated by higher financial performance.

In a related study, Sengupta (1998) investigates the link between a firm's overall disclosure quality and its cost of debt financing and finds that firms with high disclosure-quality ratings from financial analysts enjoy a lower effective interest cost. The results also indicate that the relative importance of disclosure is greater in situations where there is greater market uncertainty about the firm as reflected by the variance of the stock return. Lastly, Gebhardt *et al.* (2001) find that firms with more accurate earnings forecasts enjoy a lower implied cost of capital in valuation.

Increased following by analysts

Bhushan (1989a, 1989b) and, later on, Lang and Lundholm (1999) point out that if management's private information is not fully revealed through mandatory disclosures, voluntary disclosure lowers the cost of information acquisition for analysts and hence increases their supply of information to end users.

But supply is only one side of a market; when we look at the demand for analysts' services, the effect of voluntary disclosure is more ambiguous. Expanded disclosure potentially enables financial analysts to create valuable new information, such as superior forecasts and buy/sell recommendations, thereby increasing demand for their services. But public voluntary disclosure also pre-empts analysts' ability to distribute managers' private information to investors, leading to a decline in demand for their services.

Lang and Lundholm (1993) find that firms with more informative disclosures have larger analyst following, less dispersion in analyst forecasts, and less volatility in forecast revisions. In a related study, Healy *et al.* (1999) show that firms with improving analyst ratings of disclosure initially had lower analyst coverage than their industry peers. After the increase in disclosure, however, analyst coverage for the sample firms converges to the same level as other firms in the industry. Finally, Francis *et al.* (1998) find that there is an increase in analyst coverage for firms making conference calls.

2. ROUND-TABLE DISCUSSION

Shareholders' responsibility in monitoring

According to one capital provider, part of the current crisis of trust, especially in the U.S., is related to the traditional absence of the shareholder, and one ray of hope is that some institutional investors now become more active. In Belgium, the tradition of reference shareholders is weakening and, unlike in the U.S., the increasingly important institutional shareholders are not ready to take up their role in the relation between the shareholder and the board. The institutional shareholder, being primarily concerned about diversification of risk, does not have enough information or time to monitor and steer the policies of the many firms in which (s)he has a smallish stake. What matters is in the return on investment.

Another capital provider agrees, but adds that two more concepts related to this investment are relevant: trust and responsibility. In the U.S. the main shareholders have fiduciary duties towards all shareholders, as they have the power to appoint the majority of the directors. In Belgium this fiduciary duties are only weakly present. The larger shareholder should nevertheless participate in the shareholders' meeting, otherwise he/she is economically or ethically co-responsible even if, legally speaking, there is no problem whatsoever. But other discussants from the capital-markets panel disagree. Big shareholders should not be expected to bear all monitoring costs while getting only a *pro rata* part of the benefits. In addition, the law does not permit significant intervention by a mutual fund or an insurance company in the firm's policy, unless interests of shareholders seem to be violated beyond reasonable doubt. Thus, the statement that large investors should or will do the monitoring may be too optimistic.

Does IAS provide more transparency and may it therefore induce public trust?

There appears to be a general concern about the implementation of IAS. Some of our executives argue that IAS is made for a particular type of companies, and problems will arise when IAS has to be implemented in other type of firms. Some executives also think auditors do not have enough expertise concerning IAS. Related to the public-trust issue, the press may and will ask questions concerning the change in value of assets under IAS' valuation rules. Executives agree, by and large, that the introduction of IAS is not beneficial for the credibility of figures and forecasts.

Another executive traces the public-trust crisis partially to the fact that impact and consequences of figures and results are not always clear to the private investors. IAS will not solve this problem. It will be difficult to create a transparent firm with IAS, because the income figures will differ too much from the familiar traditional results. The major problem with IAS is it clashes with companies' predilection for hidden reserves, which can later be used to stabilize the results and hence also, it is hoped, the market price. The IAS principle of fair-value reporting is not compatible with this.

Stepping back for a wider perspective, one discussant reminds us that the attitude of people is more important than the rules. The problem is that society may want to impose more rules as a substitute for trust in the ethical value of persons. But public trust cannot be achieved by rules only.

Does voluntary disclosure increase the value of the firm?

Even though Table 21 seems to indicate substantial agreement among board members, during the debate these discussants turned out to be less than fully convinced whether disclosure is always recommendable. Some argue that the better the perspective of the firm, the more transparent the firm can afford to be, because the firm then is able to credibly make certain promises. But if a firm is performing poorly, transparency will make investors revise their valuations downward. The problem is that an asymmetric strategy (trumpeting the good news, hiding the bad) is unethical and untenable. Thus, the argument concludes, it is better to consistently retain some information, whether good or bad. But not all board members agree with the above; one argues that if there is a problem, non-transparency cannot preserve value for a firm in the long run anyway, because sooner or later the problem will be publicly known. Another board member adds that when not just bad news is surfacing but also a cover-up operation, the reaction is even worse. More in general, firms will trigger negative reactions if investors perceive the firm as not sufficiently transparent.

Table 23: Corporate disclosure and the value of the firm

"Voluntary disclosure increases shareholder value."				
	Agree	Disagree	Depends	Blank
Board of directors	6/7	0/7	0/7	1/7
Executive Committee	10/14	1/14	0/14	3/14
Capital providers	6/9	1/9	1/9	1/9
External auditors	9/11	1/11	0/11	1/11
Academics	5/8	1/8	0/8	2/8

Most board members agree that there should be a high degree of consistency in the disclosure policy of the firm. A change in reporting, for instance, may be interpreted as a signal that there is something worth covering up in the firm. The worse the firm performs, the more words it will need to convince people that all is well. Transparency should be seen as part and parcel of doing business, instead of being used just as a promotional tool for the stock. The key epithets related to transparency should be consistency and coherence in the long run.

By and large, also our capital-market people agree with the statement that transparency adds value, as can be checked in Table 23, but they also add that information that might be interesting to the competitors should not be disclosed. A code of conduct can help establish transparency in a firm. For example, clear rules should be in place to prevent insider trading; there should be transparency toward outsiders about those rules; and also the board should know who is authorized to do what.

A capital provider ripostes that transparency is not necessarily beneficial. What is important is the relevance of disclosure. The firm should disclose all relevant information and this information should be accessible to everyone, but there can also be too much information. He also asserts that quarterly reporting stimulates manipulation of figures. Auditors agree. They also favor more regulation. Tautologically, they argue, the problem with voluntary disclosure is that management can disclose what they wish. In the case of a financial statement a good directive is preferable over voluntary disclosure. Otherwise there is a risk that disclosure becomes confined to just good-news shows.

Should value reporting be mandatory?

One of the investors states that relevance should be the key factor to decide whether information should be published. Another problem with mandatory disclosure is that certain accounting valuations can be done in very different ways, which again may lead to manipulations. Consequently, there should first be very clear definitions, without room for manipulations or opportunistic choices.

Auditors agree with this view and think it is difficult to imagine that, by themselves, companies will consistently report about non-financial criteria (like innovation, or costumers). There is of course a measurement problem related to this type of disclosure. In many of these cases common standards are not specified, what makes it difficult to compare. An auditor warns that the introduction of more soft, non-financial standards would make the role of the auditor more risky and it would widen the expectations gap. Another argues that there may be a role for both more external certification and more regulation.

This wraps up the discussion about disclosure. In the next chapter, we provide information about the actual state of disclosure among Belgium's larger listed companies.

3. CONCLUSIONS

Demand for disclosure arises from information asymmetry and agency conflicts between managers and outside investors, which impede the efficient allocation of resources in a capital market. Transparency and disclosure potentially play an important role in mitigating these problems. Empirical research has mainly focused on two fields of research, the forces favouring or opposing increased disclosure and the economic benefits from increased disclosure. Six forces have been identified: capital-market transactions, corporate-control contest, stock compensation, litigation, proprietary costs and management talent signalling. As some forces will push managers towards more disclosure and others towards less, the optimum level of disclosure is determinant by the trade-off of lower capital cost and litigation cost against higher proprietary cost and incentive cost. Another field of research has focused on the economic gains from increased disclosure. There is consistent evidence that increased disclosure increases stock liquidity, reduces the cost of capital and of debt and increases information intermediation. Participants at the round table sessions also fully agree that disclosure increases shareholder value. Their opinions related to the impact of transparency on the cost of capital and of debt is however less unanimous.

REFERENCES

Aboody, D. and R. Kasznik. 2000. CEO stock option awards and the timing of corporate voluntary disclosures. *Journal of Accounting and Economics* 29: 73-100.

Ajinkya, B. and M. Gift. 1984. Corporate managers' earnings forecasts and symmetrical adjustments of market expectations. *Journal of Accounting Research* (Autumn):425 444.

Altman, E.I. 1991. *Distressed Securities: Analyzing and Evaluating Market Potential and Investment Risk.* Chicago: Probus.

Baginski, S. and J. Hassell. 1990. The market interpretation of management earnings forecasts as a predictor of subsequent financial analyst forecast revision. *The Accounting Review* 65: 175-190.

Baginski, S. P., J. M. Hassell, and W. A. Hillison. 2000. Voluntary causal disclosures: Tendencies and capital market reaction. *Review of Quantitative Finance and Accounting* 15: 371-389.

Barry, C., and S.J. Brown. 1985. Differential information and security market equilibrium. *Journal of Financial and Quantitative Analysis* 20(4): 407-422.

Barth, M., W. Beaver, and W. Landsman. 1998. Relative valuation roles of equity book value and net income as a function of financial health. *Journal of Accounting and Economics* 25: 1-34.

Barth, M.E. and A.P. Hutton. 2000. *Information intermediaries and the pricing of accruals.* Working Paper, Stanford University (Stanford, CA).

Bhushan, R. 1989a. Collection of information about publicly traded firms: Theory and evidence. *Journal of Accounting and Economics* 11, 183-207.

Bhushan, R. 1989b. Firm characteristics and analyst following. *Journal of Accounting and Economics* 11: 255-275.

Botosan, C.A. 1997. Disclosure Level and the Cost of Equity Capital. *The Accounting Review* 72: 323-349.

Brown, L. and M. Rozeff. 1978. The superiority of analyst forecasts as measures of expectations:evidence from earnings. *Journal of Finance* 33: 1-16.

Brown, P., G. Foster, and E. Noreen. 1985. Security analyst multi-year earnings forecasts and the capital market. *Studies in Accounting Research* 21.

Brown, L., P. Griffin, R. Hagerman, and M. Zmijewski. 1987. Security analyst superiority relative to univariate time-series models in forecasting quarterly earnings. *Journal of Accounting and Economics* 9: 61-87.

Brown, L. 1997. Analyst forecasting errors: Additional evidence, *Financial Analysts' Journal*, Nov/Dec: 81-88.

Chen, S., M.L. Defond and C.W. Park. 2001. Voluntary disclosure of balance sheet information in quarterly earnings announcements. http://ssrn.com/abstract=216469

Darrough, M. and N. Stoughton. 1990. Financial disclosure policy in an entry game. *Journal of Accounting and Economics* 12: 219-244.

Darrough, M.N. 1993. Disclosure policy and competition: Cournot vs. Bertrand, *Accounting Review* 68: 534-561.

Dodd, P., N. Dopuch, R. Holthausen, and R. Leftwich. 1984. Qualified audit opinions and stock prices: Information content, announcement dates, and concurrent disclosures. *Journal of Accounting and Economics* 6 (1): 3-39.

Dodd, P., R. Holthausen and R. Leftwich. 1986. Abnormal stock returns associated with media disclosures of 'subject to' qualified audit opinions. *Journal of Accounting and Economics* 8 (2): 93-118.

Dopuch, N., R. Holthausen, and R. Leftwich. 1986. Abnormal stock returns associated with media disclosures of 'subject to' qualified audit opinions. *Journal of Accounting and Economics* 8 (June): 93-117.

Diamond, D. and R. Verrecchia. 1991. Disclosure, liquidity, and the cost of capital. *Journal of Finance* 46: 1325-1359.

Dutta, S. and B. Trueman. 1997. *Optimists, pessimists, and managerial disclosures.* Working paper, University of Berckeley.

Feltham, G. and J. Xie. 1992. Voluntary financial disclosure in an entry game with continua of type. *Contemporary Accounting Research* 9: 46-80.

Francis, J., D. Philbrick and K. Schipper. 1994. Shareholder litigation and corporate disclosures. *Journal of Accounting Research* 32: 137-164.

Francis, J. and L. Soffer. 1997. The relative informativeness of analysts' stock recommendations and earnings forecast revisions. *Journal of Accounting Research* 35 (2): 193-212.

Francis, J., J. Hanna and D. Philbrick. 1998. Management communications with securities analysts, *Journal of Accounting and Economics* 24: 363-394

Frankel, R., M. Johnson and D.J. Skinner. 1997. *An Empirical Examination of Conference Calls as Voluntary Disclosure Medium.* Working Paper, University of Michigan.

Frost, C. 1997. Disclosure policy choices of UK firms receiving modified audit reports. *Journal of Accounting and Economics* 23 (July): 163-87.

Gigler, F. 1994. Self-enforcing voluntary disclosures. *Journal of Accounting Research* 32: 224-240.

Gilson, S. 1989. Management turnover and financial distress. *Journal of Financial Economics* (December):241-262.

Givoly, D. and J. Lakonishok. 1979. The information content of financial analysts' forecasts of earnings: Some evidence on semi-strong efficiency. *Journal of Accounting and Economics* 2: 165-186.

Givoly, D. 1982. Financial analysts' forecasts of earnings: A better surrogate for market expectations. *Journal of Accounting and Economics* 4 (2): 85-108.

Han, J., J. Wild, and K. Ramesh. (1989). Managers' earnings forecasts and intra-industry information transfers. *Journal of Accounting and Economics* 11 (February): pp. 3-34.

Hassell, J., R. Jennings and D. Lasser. 1988. Management earnings forecasts: Their usefulness as a source of firm-specific information to security analysts. *The Journal of Financial Research* 11: 303-320.

Healy, P. and K. Palepu. 1993. The effect of firms' financial disclosure strategies on stock prices. *Accounting Horizons* 7: 1-11.

Healy, P. and K. Palepu. 1995. The challenges of investor communications: The case of CUC International, Inc. *Journal of Financial Economics* 38: 111-41.

Healy, P., A. Hutton and K. Palepu. 1999. Stock performance and intermediation changes surrounding sustained increases in disclosure. *Contemporary Accounting Research* 16: 485-520.

Holder-Webb L. 2003. *Strategic Use of Disclosure Policy in Distressed Firms*. Working paper University of Wisconsin-Madison

Hutton, A.P., G.S. Miller and D.J. Skinner. 2003. *The Role of Supplementary Statements with Management Earnings Forecasts*. Working paper.

Jennings, R. 1987. Unsystematic security price movements, management earnings forecasts, and revisions in consensus analyst earnings forecasts, *Journal of Accounting Research* 24: 90-110.

Kasznik, R. and B. Lev. 1995. To warn or not to warn: Management disclosures in the face of an earnings surprise. *The Accounting Review* 70: 113-134.

Kim, O. and R. Verrecchia. 1994. Market liquidity and volume around earnings announcements. *Journal of Accounting and Economics* 17: 41-68.

Kreps, D. 1990. *A course in microeconomic theory*. Princeton University Press, Princeton, NJ.

Kothari, S.P. 2001. Capital markets research in accounting. *Journal of Accounting and Economics* 31: 105-231.

Lang, M. and R. Lundholm. 1993. Cross-sectional determinants of analysts ratings of corporate disclosures. *Journal of Accounting Research* 31: 246-271.

Lang, M. and R. Lundholm. 1997. *Voluntary disclosure during equity offerings: Reducing information asymmetry or hyping the stock?* Working Paper, University of Michigan (Ann Arbor, MI).

Lang, M. and R. Lundholm. 1999. Corporate disclosure policy and analyst behaviour. *The Accounting Review* 71: 467-493.

Leuz, C. and R. Verrecchia, 2000, The economic consequences of increased disclosure, *Journal of Accounting Research* 38: 91-124.

Lys, T and S. Sohn. 1990. The association between revisions of financial analysts' earnings forecasts and security price changes. *Journal of Accounting and Economics* 13: 341-364.

Matsumoto, D. 2000. *Management's incentives to avoid negative earnings surprises*. Working Paper, Harvard Business School (Boston, MA).

McGough, R. and A. Podd. 1999. Some investors criticize incomplete profit reports. *The Wall Street Journal* (August 3).

Merton, R.C. 1987. A simple model of capital market equilibrium with incomplete information. *The Journal of Finance* 42: 483-510.

Newman, P. and R. Sansing. 1993. Disclosure policies with multiple users. *Journal of Accounting Research* 31: 92-113.

Noe, C. 1999. Voluntary disclosures and insider transactions. *Journal of Accounting and Economics* 27: 305-27.

Ohlson, J. 1995. Earnings, Book Values, and Dividends in Security Valuation. *Contemporary Accounting Research* (Spring): 661-687.

Ou, J.A. and S.H. Penman. 1989. Financial statement information and the prediction of stock returns. *Journal of Accounting and Economics* 11: 295-329.

Piotroski, J. 1999. *The Impact of Newly Reported Segment Information on Market Expectations and Stock Prices.* Working paper, University of Michigan.

Rogers, J.L. and P.C. Stocken. 2003. *Credibility of Management Forecasts.* Working Paper, University of Pennsylvania.

Skinner, D.J. 1994. Why firms voluntarily disclose bad news. *Journal of Accounting Research* 32: 38-60.

Skinner, D.J., 1997. Earnings disclosures and stockholders lawsuits. *Journal of Accounting and Economics* 23: 249-282.

Trueman, B. 1986. Why do managers voluntarily release earnings forecasts? *Journal of Accounting and Economics* 8: 53-71.

Verrechia, R. E. 1983. Discretionary Disclosure, *Journal of Accounting and Economics* 5 (3): 179-194.

Wagenhofer, A. 1990. Voluntary disclosure with a strategic opponent. *Journal of Accounting and Economics* 12: 341-364.

Warner, J., R. Watts, and K. Wruck. 1988. Stock prices and top management changes. *Journal of Financial Economics* (Jan/March): 461-492.

Watts, R. and J. Zimmerman. 1981a. *The markets for independence and independence auditors.* Working Paper, University of Rochester (Rochester, NY).

Watts, R. and J. Zimmerman. 1981b. *Auditors and the determination of accounting standards.* Working Paper, University of Rochester (Rochester, NY).

Waymire, G. 1984. Additional evidence on the information content of management earnings forecasts. *Journal of Accounting Research* (Autumn):703-718.

Welker, M. 1995. Disclosure policy, information asymmetry and liquidity in equity markets. *Contemporary Accounting Research* 11: 801-828.

Williams, P. 1996. The relation between a prior earnings forecast by management and analyst response to a current management forecast. *The Accounting Review* 71 (January): 103-13.

CHAPTER 6
REPORTING PRACTICES AMONG BELGIAN LISTED COMPANIES

co-authored with Robert Peirce, Eddy Schuermans and Peter Van den Eynde

This sixth chapter describes the voluntary-disclosure practices among Belgium's listed companies from the manufacturing, media/distribution/retail and technology sectors. From an economic perspective, voluntary disclosure can be motivated by the rising doubts and disputes about the adequacy of the current (financial) corporate-reporting model. There is an abundant literature in this field. For instance, the 1994 Jenkins report finds the standard model to be wanting and proposes an own model based on users' needs. In the same year, AICPA's Special Committee on Financial Performance likewise stressed the need for more forward-looking disclosures, and the same theme forcefully comes back in FASB's "Business reporting project", started in 1999 and finalized in 2001. The report on voluntary disclosure as formulated by the AICPA recommends improved business reporting and proposes meaningful changes to the financial reporting system (AICPA, March 2002). The SEC likewise considers imposing changes in corporate disclosure rules in a series of steps to improve the financial reporting and disclosure system. (SEC, February 2002). Next to the issue of insufficient information, also the problem of misleading information has gained attention. The more recent scandals have, of course, brought doubts about the adequacy of the current financial reporting model very much to the fore, but also the issue of earnings management is much older, as shown for instance in Sir Arthur Levitt's 1998 report.

The issue is not just a conceptual or academic one. Doubts about the adequacy and reliability of information arguably lead to lower stock-market values. Many firms surely feel that their shares are undervalued, and see more extensive disclosure on non-financial performance measures as a way to help increase the usefulness and value of corporate reporting for investors, thus decreasing information asymmetry and reducing the undervaluation of stock.

1. INTRODUCING OUR SAMPLE: BELGIAN LISTED NON-FINANCIALS

The population we start from consists of all companies that meet both of the following criteria: being listed on the Brussels Stock exchange in the year 2000, and belonging to one of the following industries: manufacturing, technology, retail, distribution and media. Thus, we deliberately exclude companies from the financial industry, as well as energy and holding companies, even though this restriction seriously reduces our population. Companies in these omitted sectors have very different businesses and balance sheets, and are often much more regulated; so they are likely to behave uninformatively different from industrials and non-financial service companies.

From this population we pick a sample of 48 companies. Table 24 lists them, classified into our three industry groupings – manufacturing, technology and, lastly, retail, distribution & media – along with their NACE-BEL industry codes and year-end market capitalizations.

Our main objective is to come up with a quantitative measure of how complete the information is that is voluntarily provided by these companies on matters relevant for valuation and risk assessment. The structure and implementation of our reporting index is described in the next Section.

2. OUR VALUE AND RISK REPORTING INDEX

Our survey ignores mandatory disclosures – mainly the familiar financial items – and focuses instead on voluntary divulgence. To assess the level of voluntary disclosure of various non-financial and financial information items by our companies, we construct a "Value and Risk reporting Index" bearing on publication year 2001, as well as a variety of sub-indices.

a. STRUCTURE OF THE INDEX

The indices are based the Pricewaterhousecoopers' ValueReporting™ framework and the ValueReporter™ diagnostic tool used to evaluate a company's current level of reporting to the capital markets. ValueReporter™ provides an assessment of a company's external communications – including not just the annual and quarterly reports but also its web site, briefings, press releases and environmental and social impact reports – against the ValueReporting™ Framework, which has been developed on the basis of capital market research over the past five years. External communications are analyzed by identifying the presence or absence of qualitative and quantitative references to the specific information included in the ValueReporting™ Framework. Thus, ValueReporter™ follows the outline of the industry-specific ValueReporting™ Framework, but it drills down to the more detailed performance measures associated with each category and element of the framework. The elements of the ValueReporting™ Framework can be summarized as follows:

- market overview (competitive, regulatory and macro-economic environment), strategy (goals, objectives and governance),
- value creating activities (customers, people, innovation, brands, supply chain, environmental, social and ethical) and
- financial performance (financial position, risk profile, economic performance and segmental analysis).

Table 24: The sample: industry, market cap, and Nace-bel code

Sector	Company	Market Cap	Nace-Bel
Manufacturing	Ter Beke	13.88	1513
	Lotus Bakeries	42.06	1582
	Neuhaus	31.15	1583
	Duvel	126.86	1596
	Interbrew	15 865.23	1596
	Sioen	447.07	1754
	Vandevelde	248.27	1823
	VPK	194.98	2112
	Koramic	398.50	
	Associated Weavers	20.16	
	Ontex	454.75	2122
	Solvay	5 008.25	2413
	Tessenderlo	925.22	2413
	Recticel	253.03	2416
	Resilux	125.42	2522
	Deceuninck	350.19	2523
	Glaverbel	565.11	2611
	Bekaert	942.66	2734
	Remi Claeys	84.07	2740
	Umicore	1 024.72	2743
	Picanol	58.46	2954
Technology	IBA	25.1	3162
	Barco	991.56	3230

SECTOR	COMPANY	MARKET CAP	NACE-BEL
	Agfa Gevaert	3554.6	5155
	Econocom	108.22	5164
	Telindus	717.76	5164
	Mobistar	1 995.17	6420
	IRIS	47.94	6523
	Sait-Stento	78.35	6523
	Ubizen	329.68	7210
	Arinso International	151.48	7210
	Dolmen	129.30	7220
	Real Software	150.96	7220
	Systemat	98.04	7260
Retail, Distribution & Media	Concentra	71.72	2221
	Roularta	75.55	2213
	D'Ieteren	1 296.23	5010
	Omega Pharma	1 046.68	5146
	Colruyt	1 844.42	5211
	Delhaize	2 635.07	5211
	Brantano	180.50	5243
	Carestel	101.40	5530
	Quick	74.01	5530
	Photo Hall	47.06	6713
	Spadel	130.00	7414
	Solvus	550.92	7415
	Spector	67.17	7481
	Kinepolis	148.94	9213

Key to Table 24. For all companies, "market cap" shows the market value of the main Belgian-traded share (strips not included in market value), on December 29, 2000, in millions of Euros. For IBA we use the market value of the Australian-traded share (the Belgian-traded strip has market value of 0.1).

Table 25: Value and Risk Reporting Index: assessment sheet

Measures	Qualitative	Quantitative				
		Current Period	Prior Period	Bench-mark	Current Target	Future Target
1. Macro-economic environment 1.1 Level of Competition						
2. Strategy & Organization 2.1 Statement of LT goals						
3. Management & Performance 3.1 Internal shareholder Value metric						
4. Risk Management 4.1 Risk models and frequency of reporting						
5. Innovation 5.1 R&D expenditure						
6. Brands 6.1 Brand awareness						
7. Reputation 7.1 Product stewardship						
8. People 8.1 Employee satisfaction						
9. Supply Chain 9.1 Product quality						
10. Customers 10.1 Customer retention						

Key to Table 25. The table shows the basic layout of the assessment sheet. The complete list of items is shown in Tables 20 or 25.

Together they should provide a coherent and complete picture of the likely future of a business, against which historical financial information can be explained. It assumes that shareholder interests come first, but recognizes that long-term sustainable value is realized only if the interests of all the stakeholders are understood and addressed.

Table 25 provides a summary description of our Value and Risk Reporting Index. The complete list of questions is not included in Table 25 as it shows up again in Tables 26 and 27. The index summarizes ten categories of information items about which companies are free to disclose or not. These categories are macro-economic environment, strategy & organization, management & performance, risk management, innovation, brands, reputation, people, supply chain and, finally, customers. Note that the last six categories – innovation *sqq* – relate to the value drivers proposed in PwC's ValueReporting™.

Each of these ten categories, in turn, contains a number of specific information items. For example, specific items within the category Strategy & Organization include a statement of qualitative long-term goals, of short- and medium-term goals, and of the corporate-governance structure. Examples of specific information items within the category Risk Management include the presence of risk models, information on financial risks, and an assessment of environmental risks. Each individual information item in the index has its explicit definition, which is available on request.

b. IMPLEMENTATION OF THE ASSESSMENT

The Value and Risk Reporting Index number as produced for our companies is based on the assessment sheet partly shown in Table 25. This sheet is completed as follows. For each individual company two sources are thoroughly inspected: the annual report on the year 2000 and the company's website in December 2001. On the basis of these sources we rate the degree of disclosure on each specific information item by answering, by yes or no, the following questions:

does the company provide

1. qualitative information?
2. quantitative information about the current period?
3. quantitative information about the prior period?
4. a quantitative benchmark?
5. a current quantitative target?
6. a future quantitative target?

Qualitative information is defined as information in narrative form, whereas quantitative information uses numbers, statistics, percentages, graphs and the like. Obviously not all questions are applicable to all information items. For example, a quantitative target for the statement of long-term goals is not possible, as this item was defined to be qualitative, thus requiring exclusively narrative information.

From the completed worksheet we then derive a Value and Risk reporting score for all companies by allocating one point per positive answer, that is, whenever the company did provide information of that type in the annual report or in the website.

We then compute, for each company, percentage scores at three levels: first per information item within each of the ten information categories, then aggregated for each of these categories, and, lastly, an overall disclosure score.

Tautologically, 100% is the maximum feasible score, but we have no idea whether providing all that information would ever be viewed as useful by any real-world player, be it a provider or a user of information. To have at least a beginning of a feeling for what kind of score is realistically high or low, we immediately rescale, question by question, each of the raw scores by their maximum across firms. That is, for each question all of the company scores are divided by the highest score obtained by any firm on that same question. Thus, in what follows an overall score 100% is to be interpreted as having provided, for each and every question, as much information as the best-performing firm for that item.

This rescaling goes some way setting the maximum score in a realistic way. But even this rescaled number should be viewed with a lot of caution. First, any such score should be read in an ordinal and descriptive way rather than cardinal and normative. For example, a company which scores positively on four entries rather than two will double its score, but does not necessarily become twice as "good". Nor can one say that a company with an overall rating below 50% "fails" the examination in any meaningful way. One reason again is that the numbers are ordinal, not cardinal. Another reason why 50% is not the pass/fail mark is that firms are heterogeneous as to what information is relevant and what not. This heterogeneity means that our scaling procedure may give low marks even for companies that report adequately. For instance, if information A is relevant for company X but not for Y, while information B matters for company Y but not for X, then each firm that fully reports all relevant information would still get only 50%, under our procedure. To help cope with this and recalibrate the scales, we do provide best-practice figures in section 3.4 below.

3. RESULTS

Here's a list of questions we want to discuss in this section: what categories of information do generally receive a lot of attention, how much heterogeneity is there across firms, how do the best-performing firms fare, is there any noticeable industry effect, and what individual items seem to be perceived as quite hot or ice cold. Detailed results are provided in the Table 26. To facilitate interpretation we have condensed some key results into Tables 27, 28 and 29. We start with a discussion of the central values, viz. the mean and median scores as set out in Table 27.

a. WHICH ITEMS GET MOST ATTENTION, WHICH LEAST?

The row labeled "average", in Table 27, provides the average percentage scores per category of information item for all companies in the sample. The average company in the sample reports just 20.64% of what a theoretical firm would have done that matched, for each and every question, the best company. One possible reason for this low-looking score, as we mentioned, is that firms may be quite heterogeneous as to the type of information that is deemed to be relevant.

There is a wide variability across the ten categories, though. The average degree of voluntary disclosure on each of the information items is shown in Table 28 (in decreasing order of magnitude of the mean score). The clear lead performers are Strategy & Organization, and Management & Performance. "People" comes in as a good third, followed by Macro information and its implications for the company. We note that the bottom half, the five items with the lowest grades, includes four of the value drivers (notably customers, brands, supply chain, innovation), next to risk-management practices and initiatives.

Table 26: Value&Risk Reporting Scores, in percent

	Measures	Manufac-turing	Tech-nology	RDM	Global average
	Macro-economic environment				
1	Level of competition	25,71	14,62	13,57	**17,97**
2	Market growth (by segment & geography)	46,19	27,69	30,00	**34,63**
3	Market share (by segment & geography)	30,00	32,31	31,43	**31,25**
4	Economic	33,33	11,54	26,43	**23,77**
5	Political	21,43	0,00	21,43	**14,29**
6	Environmental	16,67	1,54	7,14	**8,45**
7	Social	10,48	0,00	1,43	**3,97**
8	Technological	17,86	6,73	16,07	**13,55**
9	Legal	42,86	26,92	35,71	**35,16**
	TOTAL	**26,32**	**13,68**	**18,65**	**19,55**
	Strategy & Organization				
10	Statement of LT goals ('Mission Statement')	100,00	80,77	78,57	**86,45**
11	Statement of ST/MT objectives (by segment)	88,10	69,23	78,57	**78,63**
12	Have targets been set for the ST/MT objectives?	21,43	24,62	25,71	**23,92**
13	Business segmentation + changes	38,10	30,77	37,14	**35,34**
14	Corporate governance model	95,24	76,92	96,43	**89,53**

	Measures	Manufac-turing	Tech-nology	RDM	Global average
15	Detailed corporate governance information	92,86	76,92	89,29	**86,36**
16	Risk Management Policy	28,57	11,54	28,57	**22,89**
17	Communication and Disclosure Policies	52,38	19,23	25,00	**32,20**
18	Stakeholder Engagement	73,81	19,23	42,86	**45,30**
19	Environmental Performance	24,29	6,92	15,00	**15,40**
20	Social Performance	61,90	7,69	28,57	32,72
	TOTAL	**44,00**	**29,26**	**37,27**	**36,84**
	Management & Performance				
21	Internal Shareholder Value Metrics (EVA...)	11,11	0,00	1,19	**4,10**
22	Return on Equity	56,35	26,92	26,19	**36,49**
23	Total Shareholder return	36,90	28,85	25,89	**30,55**
24	Earnings per share	65,08	56,41	48,81	**56,77**
25	Segmental financial indicators	60,12	54,81	54,46	**56,46**
26	Working Capital	36,31	34,62	15,18	**28,70**
27	Capital Expenditure	47,22	37,82	37,50	**40,85**
	TOTAL	**44,97**	**35,19**	**30,95**	**37,04**
	Risk management				
28	Risk models & frequency of reporting	8,84	1,10	4,08	**4,67**
29	Risk responsibility	28,57	0,00	14,29	**14,29**
30	Financial risks	17,99	5,98	6,35	**10,11**
31	Compliance risks	19,05	3,85	21,43	**14,77**
32	Environmental risks	29,23	2,50	11,67	**14,47**
33	Health and Safety risks	21,90	3,08	2,86	**9,28**
34	Technology risks	5,24	1,54	2,86	**3,21**
35	Process risks	14,29	10,26	19,05	**14,53**
36	Change management	15,48	0,00	7,14	**7,54**
	TOTAL	**15,50**	**2,87**	**7,51**	**8,62**

Table 26 Cont'd

	Measures	Manu-facturing	Tech-nology	RDM	Global average
	Value drivers – innovation				
37	R&D Expenditure	28,57	27,69	10,00	**22,09**
38	Contribution from new products	15,48	0,00	9,82	**8,43**
39	Expected contribution from products in development	6,19	1,92	14,296	**7,47**
	TOTAL	**16,84**	**10,00**	**10,36**	**12,40**
	Value drivers – brands				
40	Brand/Corporate Name Awareness	19,84	2,56	21,43	**14,61**
41	Brand Profitability and/or Equity	5,95	0,00	1,79	**2,58**
42	Revenue protected by patent(s)	9,05	2,31	0,00	**3,79**
	TOTAL	**11,67**	**1,92**	**6,79**	**6,79**
	Value drivers – reputation				
43	Product Stewardship	17,86	3,85	8,04	**9,91**
44	Health and safety performance	24,29	6,92	1,43	**10,88**
45	Third Party ratings and awards	64,29	65,38	39,29	**56,32**
	TOTAL	**25,71**	**11,54**	**7,86**	**15,04**
	Value drivers – people				
46	Employee satisfaction	18,25	17,95	3,57	**13,26**
47	Investment in training	28,57	25,64	30,95	**28,39**
48	Employee profiles	26,67	24,62	22,86	**24,71**
	TOTAL	**24,89**	**23,08**	**19,81**	**22,59**
	Value driver – supply chain				
49	Product quality	14,29	9,23	9,29	**10,93**
50	Process quality	18,25	6,41	11,90	**12,19**
51	Supplier dependence	15,48	1,92	10,71	**9,37**
	TOTAL	**15,71**	**6,92**	**10,36**	**11,00**
	Value drivers – customer				
52	Customer loyalty / retention	0,00	3,85	8,93	**4,26**
53	Customer satisfaction	14,29	21,54	11,43	**15,75**
54	of New customers vs. repeat sales	0,00	23,08	0,00	**7,69**
	TOTAL	7,14	14,62	9,29	**10,35**
	TOTAL VALUE DRIVERS	18,85	11,16	11,03	**13,68**
	GRAND TOTAL	**26,94**	**16,53**	**18,46**	**20,64**

Table 27: Descriptive statistics for all-firm average scores per information category

	Value drivers									
	Macro environ-ment	Strategy and orga-nization	Manage-ment and performance	Risk manage-ment	Innova-tion	Brand	Reputa-tion	People	Supply chain	Customer base
avg	19.55	36.84	37.04	8.62	12.40	6.79	15.04	22.59	11.00	10.35
median	15.97	34.78	37.96	3.39	7.14	5.00	10.00	18.18	10.00	10.00
stdev	14.97	18.45	15.45	13.69	16.44	10.67	17.73	14.59	11.08	13.13
coef var	0.72	0.50	0.40	1.40	1.26	1.40	1.06	0.64	0.94	1.34
min	4.17	10.86	11.11	0.00	0.00	0.00	0.00	0.00	0.00	0.00
Q1	11.11	26.01	25.93	0.00	3.57	0.00	5.00	13.64	5.00	0.00
Q2	15.97	34.78	37.96	3.39	7.14	5.00	10.00	18.18	10.00	10.00
Q3	26.39	41.30	48.15	13.98	15.71	10.00	21.25	28.41	15.00	20.00
max	91.67	100.00	83.33	62.71	92.86	50.00	80.00	72.73	55.00	60.00
# zeroes	0	0	0	15	8	20	10	3	8	23
top 10	**42.36**	**66.30**	**59.26**	**31.19**	**36.86**	**23.50**	**43.00**	**44.09**	**28.00**	**29.00**

Key to Table 27. "avg" refers to average. stdev to standard deviation. coef var to coefficient of variation, that is, standard deviation divided by average. Min and max refers to the lowest and highest observations. aQ1-3 to the first, second and third quartiles, that is, the scores that separate the bottom-ranked quarter of firms from the second group, the second from the third, and the third group from the top quarter, respectively. # zeroes lists the number of zero observations. Top 10 shows the average score across the ten best performances for that category.

Here at least there is a systematically huge gap between what the average firm does relative to the best-performing player.

A ranking on the basis of the medians produces virtually the same results (see again Table 28). The biggest downward movers, whose average seems to be have been favorably influenced by a few upward outliers, is customer base (see its rank 8 for the mean, 5 for the median). Two more items – supply chain and innovation – jump up or down two spots. But all these reshufflings remain confined to the bottom half, and value drivers remain over-represented in that lower category even when we look at medians rather than means.

b. PLENTY OF VARIABILITY ACROSS FIRMS

Central numbers. like averages and medians. are not everything; there is, of course, a considerable amount of across-firm heterogeneity within each category. Table 25 contains some intuitive measures of variability, like the highest and lowest individual scores, and the first and third quartile – that is, the scores that separate the bottom-ranked quarter of firms from the middle group, and the middle group from the top quarter, respectively. Also the standard deviation is provided, the statistician's work-horse measure of variability.

Table 28: Mean- and median-ranked scores, all companies, for the information categories

	Mean		Median	
	score	rank	score	rank
Management and performance	37.04%	1	0.3796	1
Strategy and organisation	36.84%	2	0.3478	2
People	22.59%	3	18.18%	3
Macro environment	19.55%	4	15.97%	4
Reputation	15.04%	5	10.00%	5
Innovation	12.40%	6	7.14%	8
Supply chain	11.00%	7	10.00%	5
Customer base	10.35%	8	10.00%	5
Risk management	8.62%	9	3.39%	9
Brand	6.79%	10	5.00%	10

Typically, standard deviations are quite large relative to the mean; that is, the coefficient of variation exceeds unity. This is relatively less the case for categories where the average performance is better. In other words, for items where the typical firm does well, the percentage heterogeneity across firms is lower. Note also how the larger coefficients of variation tend to go hand in hand with frequent zero entries. In two categories, notably customer relations and brand strength, almost half of the companies do not even provide any information at all, and also for risk management absolute silence reigns among more than one quarter of the companies. Recall that these are aggregate numbers for the entire category of risk-management items, not scores on individual items within the category,

c. GOOD PRACTICE AND BEST PRACTICE

We have already stressed that our scores are to be read as ordinal and descriptive rather than cardinal and normative, That is, we do not mean to signal that a below-50 rating is a failure and that a 30-rated company is twice as good in producing information as a 15-rated one. Rescaling each score as a fraction of the best score ever obtained for that question already helps us to interpret the numbers, but this procedure is heavily influenced by the top performer. To verify the robustness of our scale and possibly obtain a better feeling for what is surely a good rate, in the sense of the type of score obtained by top performers, we now look at the mean assessment of the best ten companies for each item, and then judge the average firm using that standard. Table 29 contains the results for the top-10 performers under the label "local top-10". (We justify the label "local" below.) The spider diagrams in Figure 1 provide the same information graphically.

Table 29: Mean score for the information categories: all companies versus top performers

	Local top-10		All firms		Gen top-10		Top scorer	
	mean	rank	mean	rank	mean	rank	mean	rank
Strategy and organization	66.30	1	36.84	2	60.65	1	100.0	1
Management and performance	59.26	2	37.04	1	56.85	2	77.78	5
People	44.09	3	22.59	3	30.45	5	72.73	6
Reputation	43.00	4	15.04	5	36.00	4	80.00	4
Macro environment	42.36	5	19.55	4	36.53	3	91.67	3
Innovation	36.86	6	12.40	6	23.93	7	92.86	2
Risk management	31.19	7	8.62	9	27.63	6	62.71	7
Customer	29.00	8	10.35	8	17.00	9	50.00	9
Supply chain	28.00	9	11.00	7	18.50	8	55.00	8
Brand	23.50	10	6.79	10	14.50	10	50.00	9

Key to Table 29. In the column "local top 10", we report the mean score for the ten companies that did best in that specific category. Categories are ranked on the basis of that number. so that the rank in the second column of figures tautologically rises from 1 to 10. Under "all firms" we show, for each category, the mean score obtained by all firms; the corresponding ranks are those obtained if these all-firm mean scores would be arrayed from large to small. Under "gen. top-10", short for general top-10, we show the mean scores for the (constant) group of ten companies that did best in terms of overall score rather than the best 10 per separate category; next to them again their internal ranking. Lastly, we show the individual scores and ranks obtained by the top performing individual company.

Figure 1

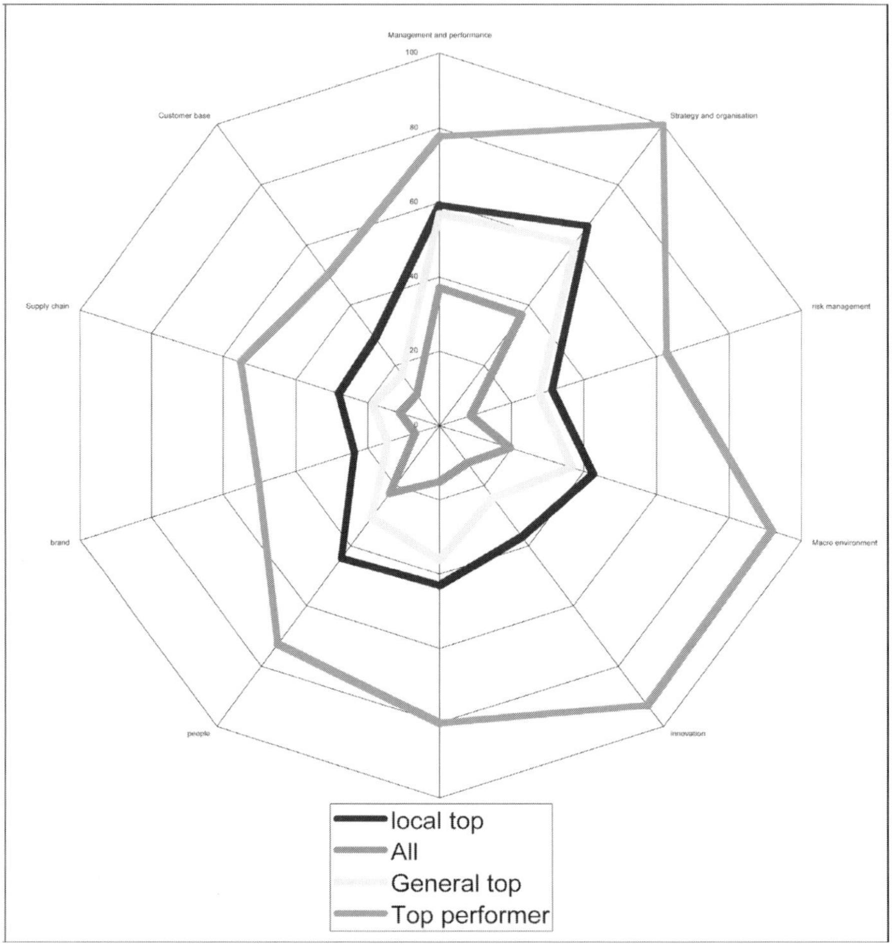

Key to Figure 1. The spider diagram displays the scores of three groups of firms and one individual company. The scores labeled "local top". refer to the mean score for the ten companies that did best in that specific category. Categories are ranked on the basis of that number. so that the curve for this set tautologically spirals inward when we move clockwise through the criteria. The group "all firms" contains. for each axis. the mean score obtained by all firms. Under "general top". short for general top-10. we show the mean scores for the (constant) group of ten companies that did best in terms of overall score rather than the best 10 per separate category. Lastly. we show the individual scores and ranks obtained by the top performing individual company.

We notice broad similarities between average and local best-practice performance. For all items, ranks for the top firms change by at most two positions relative to ranks for all firms. The six value drivers remain clear laggards. and the two top runners are still Management & Performance and Strategy & Organization, just like in the general-average-based ranking.

It could be argued that our top-10 criterion may still set the standard unattainably high, in the sense that for each of the ten categories separately we have hand-picked the ten companies that do best in that very category – hence our label, the "local" top 10. In that light, it would be interesting to know how well the "general" top-10 is faring, that is, the top group selected once and for all on the basis of the overall score instead of being lined up for each category separately. The results for the general top-10 are also shown in Table 29.

Again, rank orders hardly ever change by more than two positions. Risk Management is the sole exception, jumping three spots up. This suggests more heterogeneity across firms. There could be a two-way causality behind the relative rise of Risk Management as a reporting item. Since risk is a comparative newcomer, at least as a reporting item, companies that have opted for complete disclosure would easily do quite well relative to other companies for this otherwise neglected area. On the other hand, companies that are subject to more risks than the average firm may feel the need to generally communicate better. In the absence of any objective and comprehensive measure of risk, we cannot disentangle the two possible effects.

The mean scores for the general top-10 are not drastically below those for the local top-10. That is, it is possible to do quite respectably, by local top-10 standards, in a consistent way. We have mentioned that heterogeneity of needs – the demand side – may be one reason behind the "low"-looking general averages, rather than heterogeneity of supply – the idea that some firms care about stakeholders while others don't. However, what we see now is that there is not so much heterogeneity between top-performing firms: they tend to do well on many categories rather than excel exceptionally on just a few. This suggests that the demand side cannot be responsible for all or even most of the heterogeneity: also the company's attitude matters a lot.

To further illustrate the claim that some companies do systematically outperform on virtually all fronts we add, in the rightmost part of Table 30, the scores for the top-performing individual company. In relative terms, the company gives somewhat less attention to Risk Management and especially People than do its lesser fellow firms. In absolute terms, however, the winner easily and consistently outscores the local top 10 – even for the People item – and it usually does so by a very wide margin. Despite the odd bald patch among the value drivers, this company seems to be exceptionally and laudably systematic in its communication policies.

Let us return to the initial question as to how the average firm fares relative to a feasible best-practice benchmark. The inevitable conclusion seems to be that the typical firm stays far beyond the level of information that can be achieved with a reasonable effort. This, of course, raises a new issue: if companies would mend their ways and increase the scope of communication. in what areas is there most to be done? In the next section we report on popular and unpopular individual information items, that is, the types of information within categories.

d. DISCLOSURE RATES ON INDIVIDUAL ITEMS

Also as to the individual information items we note a great deal of heterogeneity and right-skewness (a predominance of upward outliers rather than downward ones) across items, with very complete divulgence for a few items and very poor disclosure for rather more of them.

Table 30 shows the individual questions. grouped and ranked on the basis of the number of firms that totally ignore them. For instance. only three firms stay completely silent on their corporate-governance model. which makes it the most often-discussed item. We form two categories – firstly, items that were discussed by at least half of the 48 firms, and then items that were discussed by less than half. Within each category, we rank by the number of blanks we drew. The top-10 Greatest Hits contain few surprises. We see the importance of corporate governance issues confirmed, coming ahead even of the corporate goals and of vital non-mandatory financial items like planned investments in physical assets and R&D, segmental financial indicators, and earnings per share (EPS). The relatively low rank of EPS may be a bit of a surprise, to some. Market share and growth are obvious members of the top-10 items, too. The less popular items are almost exclusively drawn from the boxes of the least popular value drivers. It is not clear, of course, whether this means that companies regard these items as irrelevant, or deem the issue to be too sensitive, or never thought about mentioning it in the first place.

Table 30: Most and least often discussed individual information items

	Most often discussed		Least often discussed
3	Corporate governance model	25	Brand/Corporate Name Awareness
	Detailed corporate governance information		Customer satisfaction
	Capital Expenditure	26	Employee satisfaction
4	Market share (by segment & geography)		Process quality
	Statement of LT goals	27	Technological
	Statement of ST/MT objectives (by segment)		Social Performance
	Business segmentation + changes	28	Legal issues
5	Market growth (by segment & geography)		Communication and Disclosure Policies
6	Segmental financial indicators		Health and safety performance
7	Earnings per share	29	Financial risks
8	Level of competition		Health and Safety risks
9	Economic issues	30	Product Stewardship
10	R&D Expenditure	32	Environmental issues
11	Employee profiles	33	Risk Management Policy
14	Total Shareholder return	34	Compliance risks
15	Return on Equity	35	Process risks
16	Investment in training		Supplier dependence
17	Product quality	36	Contribution from new products
19	Environmental Performance	39	Political issues
	Working Capital		Revenue protected by patent(s)
	Environmental risks	40	Risk responsibility
	Third Party ratings and awards		Change management
20	Set segments' targets for ST/MT objectives?		Expected contribution from products in development
	Stakeholder Engagement		
		41	Risk models & frequency of reporting
		42	Social issues
		43	Technology risks
		44	Internal Shareholder Value Metrics (*e.g.* EVA)
			Customer loyalty / retention
		45	Brand Profitability and/or Equity
			% of New customers vs. repeat sales

Key to Table 30. The individual information items are ranked by the number of firms that stay utterly silent on the item – number shown next to the item. Thus, only three firms do not talk about corporate governance, while 45 never mention new customers versus repeat sales.

e. SECTOR DIFFERENCES

In Table 26 one also notices rather systematic differences between the average scores of the three sectors. By and large, the companies in the manufacturing sector disclose significantly more information than companies in the two other sectors: the average scores are 18.63% for the manufacturing sector, 12.32% for retail/distribution/media (RDM), and 11.35% for the Technology sector. It thus appears that companies from traditional industries are more communicative than younger companies in the Technology sector. The manufacturing sector outperforms the other two sectors quite consistently, viz. on each of the ten information categories except customers.

The interpretation of the superior performance of the manufacturing group is less obvious. Age and experience are not likely to be a major explanatory factor, since in each sector only a minority of the companies in our sample are newcomers as listed firms. Nor can one argue that the manufacturing industry is especially risk-prone and, therefore, generous with information. We see at least two possible explanations, one supply- and one demand-driven. In the supply-side view, the industrials feel the need to work harder to retain the investor's attention amidst the (then) raging dot.com madness. The demand-driven story, alternatively, argues that old-economy firms, having been active for a long time in a sector that is well understood by investors, know what information is being asked, and they respond to that. In contrast, when dealing with Hi-Tech firms investors know less well what questions to ask and how to use any information supplied by them. Low demand then generates low supply. The fact that the manufacturing firms are less different from the retail/distribution/media group than from the technology subsample is consistent with both the supply- and demand-side stories: manufacturing would normally have the most pronounced "old-economy" image, followed by retail etc, and with technology being at the other extreme.

f. SPECIFIC DISCLOSURE DIFFERENCES BETWEEN SECTORS

To close this section, we provide more details on the three pairwise comparisons for each of the ten categories as reported in Table 31.

Macro-economic environment

The manufacturing sector significantly outperforms the technology sector with respect to information provision on the items market growth, economic conditions, political situation and environmental issues. All other disclosure differences between the other sectors are not significant, unless disclosure of economic condition between Technology sector and RDM, where RDM outperforms technology.

Strategy & Organization

Again, the manufacturing sector significantly outperforms the technology sector. As to individual items, the differences between manufacturing and technology are only significant for disclosure on Communication & disclosure policies, Stakeholder engagement, Environmental performance and Social performance. The disclosure differences regarding individual items between the other sectors are only significant for social performance between manufacturing and RDM.

Management and Performance

As far as information on management and performance is concerned, there is only a significant difference between the manufacturing sector and RDM. As to individual items, the differences between manufacturing and RDM are only significant for disclosure on Return on Equity and Working Capital. Note that manufacturing also outperforms technology with respect to ROE.

Table 31: T-tests of mean differences between sector scores

Measures		M-T	M-RDM	T-RDM
	Macro-economic environment			
1	Level of competition	0.0980	0.0659	0.8631
2	Market growth (by segment & geography)	**0.0238**	0.1045	0.8088
3	Market share (by segment & geography)	0.7872	0.8733	0.9315
4	Economic	**0.0075**	0.3713	**0.0368**
5	Political	**0.0250**	1.0000	0.0537
6	Environmental	**0.0066**	0.1797	0.2974
7	Social	0.0753	0.1304	0.3356
8	Technological	0.1068	0.8349	0.1846
9	Legal	0.3195	0.6703	0.6298
	TOTAL	**0.0101**	**0.1341**	**0.1972**
	Strategy and Organization			
10	Statement of LT goals ('Mission Statement')	0.0961	0.0537	0.8822
11	Statement of ST/MT objectives (by segment)	0.1653	0.3452	0.5353
12	Have targets been set for the ST/MT objectives? (by segment)	0.7613	0.6995	0.9310
13	Business segmentation + changes	0.4183	0.9235	0.5016
14	Corporate governance model	0.1384	0.8427	0.1066
15	Detailed corporate governance information	0.1997	0.6469	0.3232

Measures		M-T	M-RDM	T-RDM
16	Risk Management Policy	0.1704	1.0000	0.2388
17	Communication and Disclosure Policies	**0.0312**	0.0821	0.7149
18	Stakeholder Engagement	**0.0004**	0.0516	0.1663
19	Environmental Performance	**0.0119**	0.2537	0.2790
20	Social Performance	**0.0000**	**0.0449**	0.1419
	TOTAL	**0.0081**	**0.3351**	**0.2162**
	Management & Performance			
21	Internal Shareholder Value Metrics (*e.g.*. EVA)	0.0896	0.1324	0.3356
22	Return on Equity	**0.0066**	**0.0107**	0.9494
23	Total Shareholder return	0.3783	0.2027	0.7381
24	Earnings per share	0.4657	0.1211	0.5657
25	Segmental financial indicators	0.6224	0.5665	0.9753
26	Working Capital	0.8690	0.0315	0.0703
27	Capital Expenditure	0.2032	0.2574	0.9704
	TOTAL	**0.0465**	**0.0118**	**0.4136**
	Risk management			
28	Risk models & frequency of reporting	0.1772	0.4284	0.2623
29	Risk responsibility	**0.0104**	0.3155	0.1648
30	Financial risks	0.0594	0.1277	0.9472
31	Compliance risks	**0.0242**	0.8358	0.1226
32	Environmental risks	**0.0163**	0.1361	0.1948
33	Health and Safety risks	**0.0035**	**0.0030**	0.9391
34	Technology risks	0.4669	0.6472	0.5993
35	Process risks	0.6402	0.6488	0.4486
36	Change management	**0.0195**	0.2925	0.1648
	TOTAL	**0.0028**	**0.1021**	**0.1974**
	Value drivers – innovation			
37	R&D Expenditure	0.9101	**0.0076**	**0.0179**
38	Contribution from new products	**0.0239**	0.4616	**0.0353**
39	Expected contribution from products in development	0.4523	0.5174	0.8155
	TOTAL	**0.2561**	**0.0847**	**0.3504**
	Value drivers – brands			
40	Brand/Corporate Name Awareness	**0.0009**	0.8526	**0.0242**
41	Brand Profitability and/or Equity	0.2340	0.4277	0.3356
42	Revenue protected by patent(s)	0.1932	0.0783	0.0821
	TOTAL	**0.0038**	**0.1924**	**0.0517**

Measures		M-T	M-RDM	T-RDM
	Value drivers – reputation			
43	Product Stewardship	**0.0364**	0.1753	0.3545
44	Health and safety performance	**0.0190**	**0.0003**	0.2838
45	Third Party ratings and awards	0.9483	0.1455	0.1707
	TOTAL	**0.0184**	**0.0017**	**0.3747**
	Value drivers – people			
46	Employee satisfaction	0.9753	**0.0165**	0.1074
47	Investment in training	0.7626	0.8225	0.6251
48	Employee profiles	0.7768	0.6606	0.7892
	TOTAL	**0.7163**	**0.3218**	**0.4512**
	Value driver – supply chain			
49	Product quality	0.3530	0.3407	0.9874
50	Process quality	0.0644	0.3373	0.2585
51	Supplier dependence	**0.0088**	0.5809	0.2614
	TOTAL	**0.0157**	**0.1695**	**0.3179**
	Value drivers – customer			
52	Customer loyalty / retention	0.1654	0.2386	0.5175
53	Customer satisfaction	0.3121	0.6817	0.1384
54	% of New customers vs. repeat sales	0.0821	0.3356	0.0829
	TOTAL	**0.0657**	**0.6769**	**0.3224**
	TOTAL VALUE DRIVERS	**0.0259**	**0.0137**	**0.6180**
	GRAND TOTAL	**0.0030**	**0.0223**	0.5894

Risk Management

Although disclosure of risk management information is generally rather poor, there are significant differences between the sectors. Manufacturing outperforms technology overall, and specifically with respect to disclosure of risk responsibility, compliance risks, environmental risks, health and safety risks and change management. Further, Manufacturing also outperforms RDM regarding the disclosure of health and safety risks.

Innovation

Overall, there are no significant disclosure differences between the sectors, but on the individual level both manufacturing and technology significantly outperform RDM with respect to disclosure of R&D expenditure. Further, Manufacturing outperforms technology with respect to brand profitability.

Brands

Overall disclosure on this information category is low and there are no significant disclosure differences between the sectors. On the individual level: both manufacturing and RDM outperform technology with respect to disclosure of brand name awareness. Manufacturing outperforms technology with respect to brand profitability.

Reputation

The manufacturing sector outperforms the two other sectors with respect to the voluntary disclosure level of this information category. As to individual items. disclosure of health & safety performance is significantly higher in the manufacturing sector as compared to both other sectors.

People

Unlike most other information categories, disclosure scores are similar in the three sectors. There is only a significant difference between the manufacturing and RDM sector as to disclosure on employee satisfaction.

Supply chain

For this information category, the manufacturing sector significantly outperforms the technology sector. This difference is mainly due to disclosure differences with respect to supplier dependence.

Customer

Unlike most other information categories, the manufacturing sector has the lowest score, but the difference with the other sectors is not statistically significant.

4. CONCLUSIONS

Our objective, in this chapter, is to picture the practices among Belgian public firms re voluntary disclosure. We provide an overall score, a subtotal for each of ten information categories, and individual scores. We likewise discuss results for the average or median firm, for the top performers, and for firms grouped by industry.

We find that only two subtotals, Management & Performance and Organization & Strategy, fare rather well almost across the board. The value drivers, in contrast, tend to come in among the lowest-ranked items, as does Risk Management. For two value drivers, Brands and Customers, around half of the companies even remain utterly silent. Across firms. there often is a pronounced right-skewness among the rankings for one subcategory.

The top-performing companies are doing spectacularly better on Risk Management, and (relatively) worse on macro information. Manufacturing firms do best, both in terms of total rating as well as on most subcategories, followed by retail/distribution/media (RDM) and then Technology. This is the ordering one expects if extra information aims at overcoming the relative lack of glamour among RDM firms and, especially, manufacturers. But it could equally well mean that investors simply know what questions to ask from traditional firms, and less so from tech companies.

CHAPTER 7 – CONCLUDING CHAPTER THE LIPPENS CODE VERSUS THE EMPIRICAL EVIDENCE

1. INTRODUCTION

Corporate Governance has been the subject of much debate by policymakers at various levels: international, transnational and national. One reason is that there is a clear link between corporate governance, investments and economic growth and performance. Good Governance is believed to build economic confidence, therefore facilitates access to external financing and plays a critical role in channelling savings to productive investment. In 2003 the European Commission launched its Action Plan on 'Modernising Company Law and Enhancing Corporate Governance in the European Union'. As Belgium is a member state of the EU, Belgian corporate governance and auditing rules cannot be looked at in isolation. At the EU level, recent initiatives have focused on two directions to achieve increased transparency: corporate-governance measures and measures relating to auditor independence. The European framework leaves room for diversity through the "comply and explain" system and is in essence principles based.

In this final chapter we will first elaborate on the major principles of the Belgian Lippens code and contrast these with the empirical evidence and Belgian practices as identified in our study.

2. THE BELGIAN CODE ON CORPORATE GOVERNANCE

In Belgium, best practice codes have been in place for listed companies since 1998, but no provision in these codes may be interpreted as derogating from Belgian Law. In 1998 the Brussels Exchanges (i.e. the Commission Cardon), The Banking and Finance Commission (CBF) as well as the Federation of Belgian Enterprises (CEB-VBO) issued *recommendations* on good corporate governance. The recommendations of the CBF related to disclosure on corporate governance, whereas the recommendations of the Brussels Exchanges and VBO rather described good corporate governance practice[10]. In particular, they pertain to the responsibilities, size, composition and working procedures of the board of directors (BOD). The Brussels Exchanges recommended in 1998, for example, that the board should not consist of more than 12 directors, and that the majority of the directors should be non-executives. Another recommendation was that part of the non-executive directors be independent of management as well as of the majority shareholders and that the company establishes an audit committee.[11]

At the initiative of the same parties who were involved in the 1998 Corporate Governance recommendations – that is, the Banking, Finance and Insurance Commission (BFIC, formerly BFC), Euronext Brussels (formerly Brussels Exchanges) and the Federation of Belgian Enterprises (FEB-VBO)) – a committee was established to draft a new code of best practice on corporate governance for all listed companies. This new code (i.e. Code Lippens) was launched in December 2004, is effective as of 2005, and is aligned with OECD principles and EU recommendations. It has a high degree of built-in flexibility as it is based on the 'comply or explain' system. Disclosure leading to transparency is an essential ingredient of the Code. Transparency is to be obtained through two different documents: the corporate-governance charter (on the corporate website) and the corporate-governance chapter (included in the annual report). The code contains three types of rules: principles, provisions and guidelines. According to the Corporate Governance Committee the nine principles form the pillars of good governance. Provisions are recommendations describing how to apply the principles, and guidelines provide guidance as to how the company should implement or interpret the provisions. The new rules in the code relate to best-practice board characteristics (independence, size, leadership, remuneration, etc.), audit committee membership characteristics, and explicitly recommend the installation of an internal audit function within the company. Note that the Code is complementary to Belgian legislation, but the BFIC recommends listed companies to disclose relevant information about their corporate governance rules and practices in accordance with provisions of the Code.

3. THE LIPPENS CODE VS. THE INTERNATIONAL EVIDENCE

In this section, we evaluate the principles in the Lippens Code, by looking at the international evidence regarding the effectiveness of various corporate governance principles. Table 32 provides an overview of those principles, provisions and guide

---

10 These are recommendations and in no way mandatory regulations. The regulation of the internal audit function within commercial banks (see CBF 1997) is an exception.

11 Other recommendations related to the responsibilities and remuneration of non-executive directors, remuneration of management and reporting and control.

lines from the Lippens Code about which the literature provides evidence regarding their effectiveness.

Table 32

Variables of interest	The Belgian Code on Corporate Governance	International Empirical Evidence
	Board of Directors	
CEO=Chair	1.5 The chairman of the board and CEO should not be the same individual.	Separation of the roles of CEO and chairman of the board is positively associated with: – Accounting performance – Dismissal CEO
Board size	2.1a The board should be small enough for efficient decision-making.	Board size is negatively associated with: – Accounting performance – Dismissal CEO
	2.2b The board should be large enough for its members to contribute experience and knowledge from different fields	Board size is positively associated with: – Earnings Management – Fraud
Board Independence	2.2b At least half the board should comprise non-executive directors and at least three of them should be independent.	No association of board independence with: – Accounting performance Negatively associated with: – Income-increasing manipulation – Fraud Positively associated with: – CEO compensation – Stock returns Mixed evidence: – Dismissal CEO – Takeovers & acquisitions

Variables of interest	The Belgian Code on Corporate Governance	International Empirical Evidence
	Audit committee	
Audit committee presence	5.2 The board should set up an audit committee to assist the board in fulfilling its monitoring responsibilities.	AC presence is negatively associated with: – Earnings management Negative or no association with: – Financial misstatements fraud
Audit committee independence	5.2./2a The board should set up an audit committee composed exclusively of non-executive directors.	AC independence is negatively associated with: – Earnings management – Financial misstatements and fraud
	5.2./2b At least a majority of its members should be independent.	
	5.2./2c The chairman of the board should not chair the audit committee.	
Audit committee role	5.2./6 The committee should discuss significant financial reporting issues with both executive management and the external auditor	AC independence is positively associated with: – Receiving going-concern audit opinion
	5.2./14 The audit committee should monitor the external auditor's independence [...]	
	5.2./17 The audit committee should review the effectiveness of the external audit process	AC presence leads to increased audit demand in Belgium
	Internal audit	
	5.2./9 An independent internal audit function should be established, [...]. If the company does not have an internal audit function, the need for one should be reviewed at least annually.	Companies with an independent audit function are more transparent in general and w.r.t. financial risk management in particular.
	External audit	
	No specific standards apply to auditors, but rather to the board and especially the audit committee which has to monitor the activities of external auditors (cfr. Appendix C, rules 5.2./13 – 18).	Higher external audit quality leads to less earnings management and more qualified audit opinions (ceteris paribus). The evidence for Belgium is consistent but weaker.

Variables of interest	The Belgian Code on Corporate Governance	International Empirical Evidence
	Transparency and disclosure	
Transparency	9.1 The company should establish a CG Charter describing all the main aspects of its corporate governance policy. 9.2 The company should state in its CG Charter that it follows the Corporate Governance Principles laid down in this Code.	Voluntary disclosure is positively associated with: – Capital-market transactions – CEO turnover in distressed firms – Stock liquidity
	5.1 The board should determine and disclose in the CG Charter the terms of reference of each committee detailing its role, composition and operation. 6.1 The board should determine and disclose the terms of reference of the executive management detailing its responsibilities, duties, powers, composition and operation. 7.2 The company should disclose its remuneration policy in its CG Charter.	Voluntary disclosure is negatively associated with: – Cost of capital – Cost of debt
	7.5 In the CG Chapter of the annual report, the company should disclose on an individual basis the amount of the remuneration and other benefits granted directly or indirectly to non-executive directors. 7.15 In the CG Chapter of the annual report, the company should disclose, on an individual basis, the amount of the remuneration and other benefits granted to the CEO. 7.16 In the CG Chapter of the annual report, the company should disclose, on a global basis, the amount of the remuneration granted to the other members of executive management. 7.17 For the CEO and the other executive managers, the CG Chapter of the annual report should disclose, on an individual basis, the number and key features of shares, share options or any other right to acquire shares, granted during the year. 7.18 The company should disclose in the CG Chapter of the annual report the main contractual terms of hiring and termination arrangements with executive managers. 8.4 The company should disclose in its CG Charter its shareholding and control structure and any cross-shareholdings exceeding 5% of the shareholdings or voting rights.	

Board characteristics

The Lippens code emphasizes the dual role of the board of directors: entrepreneurial and monitoring (reference to Lippens). In the international literature we find evidence related to three distinct board characteristics: a) separation of the functions of CEO and chairman of the board; b) board size; and c) board independence. The Lippens code very clearly indicates that the chairman of the board and the CEO should not be the same individual. In the literature, there is evidence that separation of these functions indeed leads to better accounting performance and quicker dismissal of CEO's in case of sub-standard performance. From our investigation for Belgian listed companies (see also chapter 1, Section 2), it seems that in 2003 already about 65% of the listed firms in our sample comply with this standard.

Regarding board size, the Lippens code states that boards should not be too large, but also not too small. In the literature the evidence is supportive of a negative association between board size and a) accounting performance and b) CEO dismissal. A positive association is found between board size and a) earnings management and b) fraud. Hence, the evidence is supportive of small boards. Note that in our Belgian sample, the median board consists of 9 members.

As far as board independence is concerned, the code prescribes that at least half the board should comprise non-executive directors. The evidence indicates that board independence is indeed a mechanism that constrains earnings manipulation and fraud, and hence serves a *monitoring role*. There is evidence that board independence is positively associated with CEO compensation and stock performance. There is however no evidence of a significant association with accounting performance and the link with CEO dismissal and takeover decisions is ambiguous. This suggests that there is no univocal evidence that the *entrepreneurial role* of the board is enhanced by including more outside directors. Note that on average the 2003 Belgian board consist of 40% independent members and 66,6% non-executive members.

Audit committee

The audit committee clearly serves a monitoring role. The Lippens code prescribes the installation of an audit committee. The literature provides evidence that the presence of an audit committee is negatively associated with earnings management and fraud. However, the results based on the Belgian governance and earnings-management data that we collected in this study (see also Chapter 2 for details) do not support this argument. This may mean that the mere presence of an audit committee is not sufficient to constrain earnings manipulation and fraud in Belgium.

According to the Lippens code the audit committee should consist exclusively of non-executive directors, and at least a majority of the members should be independent.

In addition the chair person of the board should not function as the chair person of the audit committee. The international empirical evidence clearly endorses these standards, as it indicates that audit committee independence is negatively associated with earnings management and financial statement fraud.

According to the Lippens code, the audit committee serves various monitoring roles relating to financial reporting, internal control and risk management, the internal audit process and the external audit process. There is not so much empirical evidence regarding the effectiveness of audit committees with respect to all these roles. There is however clear evidence that the more independent members there are in the audit committee, the higher the likelihood is of a going-concern opinion provided by the external auditor. This may mean that independent audit committees tend to be more effective in monitoring the external audit process.

Internal audit function

Appendix C of the Lippens codes states that listed companies should install an independent internal audit function, and if a company does not have one, the need for one should be reviewed at least annually. The evidence on internal audit effectiveness is rather scarce in the literature. However, a recent study for Belgium (See Willekens et al. 2005) reports that the presence of an internal audit function is associated with more disclosure about the way the company manages its financial risks.

External audit function

Although there are no rules in the Lippens code that directly apply to external auditors, the code includes rules that the audit committee should monitor the independence and activities of its external auditor. There is a rich literature (worldwide) on auditor independence and audit quality differentiation that suggests that larger auditors constrain earnings management more and issue more non-clean audit opinions, ceteris paribus. The evidence for Belgium in this regard is weaker.

Transparency

Transparency about corporate governance is a key aspect of the Lippens code, as it contains plenty of disclosure requirements related to the governance mechanisms. Even though there is not much evidence about the impact of voluntary corporate governance disclosures per se, there is a broad literature on voluntary accounting disclosures. In general the evidence is consistent with more disclosure being associated with more capital-market transactions, more CEO turnover in distressed firms, more stock liquidity, lower cost of capital and lower cost of debt.

4. THE LIPPENS CODE VERSUS THE BELGIAN EVIDENCE (PRE-LIPPENS)

In this section we focus on the empirical evidence for Belgium. Table 33 provides an overview of empirical findings in various studies that use Belgian data and the descriptive statistics from this study.

Table 33: The Belgian code versus the Belgian evidence

Belgian Corporate Governance Code	**Actual practice in 2003**	**Belgian empirical evidence**
BOARD OF DIRECTORS: **Principle 1: The Company shall adopt a clear governance structure**		
1.5 The chairman of the board and CEO should not be the same individual.	Percentage of boards where CEO and chairman are different individuals: 65%	– *No* clear association of split roles with earnings management and transparency (Willekens & Sercu, Chapter 2) – Contradictory evidence: positive association between split roles and earnings management (Willekens & Sercu Chapter 2) – *As expected*: Split roles between CEO and chairman is associated with more transparency regarding financial risk management (Willekens, Bruynseels & Heiremans, 2005)
Principle 2: The company shall have an effective and efficient board taking decisions in the corporate interest		
2.1a The board should be small enough for efficient decision-making. 2.1b The board should be large enough for its members to contribute experience and knowledge from different fields	Median size board was 9	*Opposite from expected*: Negative association of board size with earnings management (Willekens & Sercu, Chapter 2)

Belgian Corporate Governance Code	Actual practice in 2003	Belgian empirical evidence
2.2b At least half the board should consist of non-executive directors ...	Percentage on non-executive directors: 66.6%	*As expected*: Positive association of non-executive members with external audit demand (Knechel and Willekens, 2004) *No* clear association of non-executive members with with earnings management (Willekens & Sercu, Chapter 2)
... and at least three of them should be independent.	Percentage of independent board members: 40.0%	
2.7. guideline: the board should meet sufficiently regularly to discharge its duties effectively	Median number of board meetings was 6	*Opposite from expected*: Negative association of board size with transparency (Willekens & Sercu, Chapter 2)
Principle 5: The board shall set up specialised committees		
5.4. The board should set up a remuneration committee following the provisions set out in Appendix E.	In 77.1% of the sample companies there was a remuneration committee	
5.2. The board should set up an audit committee to assist the board in fulfilling its monitoring responsibilities in respect of control in the broadest sense.	In 77.1% of the sample companies there was an audit committee	Evidence for Belgium indicates that voluntary audit committee formation (pré-Lippens) is significantly positively associated with the proportion of independent directors on the board and external audit-firm size; unlike prior studies there is no association with agency costs and board size (Willekens, Vander Bauwhede and Gaeremynck, 2004).
5.3. The board should set up a nomination committee following the provisions set out in appendix D.	In 41.6% of the sample companies there was a nomination committee	

Belgian Corporate Governance Code	Actual practice in 2003	Belgian empirical evidence
Principle 6: The board shall define a clear executive management structure		
Preambule p.7. The code has been drawn up with the 'one-tier board' model in mind… 1.4. The board should decide on the executive management structure and determine the powers and duties entrusted to executive management. These should be included in the terms of reference of the board and in those of executive management.	In 75% of the sample companies there was an executive committee	
Principle 7: The company shall remunerate directors and executive managers fairly and responsibly		
7.4. Non-executive directors should not be entitled to performance-related remuneration, such as bonuses, stock related long-term incentive schemes, fringe benefits or pension benefits.	In 11.8% of companies, compensation differed between executive and non-executive board members. In 29.40% of companies all board members receive a mixture of fixed and variable compensation Note that in 5% of companies, audit committee members received a mixture of fixed and variable compensation !	

Belgian Corporate Governance Code	Actual practice in 2003	Belgian empirical evidence
7.11. An appropriate proportion of an executive manager's remuneration package should be structured so as to link rewards to corporate and individual performance, thereby aligning the executive manager's interest with the interest of the company and its shareholders.	In 20% of companies, the excom members receive only a fixed compensation. In 64% of companies excom members receive a mixture of fixed and variable compensation. In 16% of companies excom members receive only variable compensation.	
7.15. In the CG chapter of the annual report, the company, should disclose, on an individual basis, the amount of the remuneration and other benefits granted directly or indirectly to the CEO, by the company or any other undertaking belonging to the same group. This information should be disclosed with a split between: – basic remuneration – variable remuneration... – other...	0% of companies discloses individual compensation of CEO	
7.16. In the CG chapter of the annual report, the company, should disclose, on a global basis, the amount of the remuneration and other benefits granted directly or indirectly to the other members of executive management, by the company or any other undertaking belonging to the same group. This information should be disclosed with a split between: – basic remuneration – variable remuneration... – other....	66.7% discloses total compensation of Excom; 0% discloses individual compensation of Excom.	

Belgian Corporate Governance Code	Actual practice in 2003	Belgian empirical evidence
Principle 9: The board shall ensure adequate disclosure of its corporate governance.		
9.4. The company should establish a CG chapter in its annual report …	Disclosure of board rules in AR in 2003 by 89.6%	*Results as expected:* Companies that disclose/have a corporate charter exhibit less earnings management (Willekens & Sercu, Chapter 2)
AUDIT COMMITTEE		
Principle 5: see above Appendix C: this entire appendix describe the role and functioning of the audit committee	In 77.1% of companies there was an AC installed.	*No clear association*: Audit committee presence does not lead to less earnings management (Willekens & Sercu, Chapter 2) *No clear association*: Audit committee presence does not lead to more overall transparency (Willekens & Sercu, Chapter 2)
INTERNAL AUDIT FUNCTION		
5.2./9 An independent internal audit function should be established, … If the company does not have an internal audit function, the need for one should be reviewed at least annually.		*As expected*: The presence of an internal audit function leads to more transparency regarding financial risk management (Willekens, Bruynseels & Heiremans, 2005) The presence of an internal audit function leads to more transparency regarding both historical and voluntary corporate information in general, and information regarding innovation, learning and customers in particular (Willekens, Gaeremynck, Van de Gucht and Vander Bauwhede, 2005).

Belgian Corporate Governance Code	**Actual practice in 2003**	**Belgian empirical evidence**
EXTERNAL AUDIT FUNCTION		
No specific standards that apply to auditors, but rather to the board and especially the audit committee which has to monitor the activities of external auditors (cfr. Appendix C, rules 5.2./13 – 18).		*No clear association / Weak results as expected (note that this particular evidence is based on samples of non-listed firms!)*: There is no difference in auditor reporting behaviour between big 6 and other auditors for clients that subsequently go bankrupt (Gaeremynck & Willekens, 2003; Vanstraelen 2002). Big 6 auditors, however, provide more non-clean audit opinions for client that subsequently go into voluntary liquidation (Gaeremynck & Willekens, 2003) *No clear association / weak result as expected:* Big 6 auditors constrain earnings management more in large client segment (Vander Bauwhede, Willekens & Gaeremynck 2003), but not in non-listed companies (Sercu, Vander Bauwhede and Willekens 2003, Vander Bauwhede & Willekens 2004). *As expected:* there is a positive association between the presence of a big external auditor and corporate transparency (Willekens & Sercu, chapter 2)

The Board and board effectiveness in Belgium

In Belgium[12], a median board consists of 9 members, meets 6 times per year and has on average 66.6% non-executive members, and 40% independent members. The Lippens code clearly states that there should be a clear division of responsibilities between the CEO and the chair of the board. This is already the case in 65% of our sample companies. However, from the empirical evidence for Belgium, we learn that separation of these roles is not associated with less earnings management, nor with (more) overall corporate transparency, but there seems to be a positive association

[12] All descriptive statistics relate to 2003.

with transparency about financial risks and how they are managed (Willekens, Bruynseels and Heiremans 2005). The Lippens code further also states that boards should be neither too large nor too small. But the empirical evidence that is available so far, seems to indicate that larger boards leads to less earnings management (see Chapter 2). The Lippens code requires that half of the board members are non-executives and that at least three board members should be independent. The average Belgian board already meets these criteria (i.e. on average 66.6% non-executives and 40% independents, respectively). As far as the Belgian evidence is concerned, it seems that the presence of more non-executive board members triggers more external auditing in a firm (Knechel and Willekens 2004), but there is no association with earnings management (Willekens and Sercu, 2005). Finally, funnily enough, more board meetings seem to be associated with less transparency in Belgium, instead of more (see Chapter 2).

Note that the Belgian code emphasizes that disclosure of a corporate governance charter and chapter is essential. Note that 89.6% of our sample companies already disclose the rules of the board of directors in their annual reports before the Lippens Code was established. The evidence further indicates that companies that disclose or have a corporate governance charter exhibit less earnings management (see Chapter 2).

Audit committee effectiveness in Belgium

The Lippens code proposes that listed companies establish an audit committee. Further, Appendix C to the Lippens codes devotes considerable attention to the role and functioning of audit committees. Note that 77.1% of our sample companies already had an audit committee. As to the effectiveness of such a committee, there is not much evidence so far. However, the evidence that is available is not very favourable. There seems to be no association between the presence of an audit committee and earnings management, nor between the presence of an audit committee and corporate transparency (Willekens and Sercu, 2005). This evidence seems to indicate that the mere installation of an audit committee may not lead to expected monitoring result.

Internal Audit function

The Lippens code also requires that listed companies install an internal audit function. Note that about 60% of our sample companies had such a function in 2003. The evidence regarding the effectiveness of the internal audit function is more favourable compared to the audit committee function. The presence of an internal audit function seems to lead to more transparency regarding financial risk management (Willekens, Bruynseels and Heiremans 2005) and more transparency regarding both historical and voluntary corporate information in general, and information regarding innovation, learning and customers in particular (Willekens, Gaeremynck, Van de Gucht and Vander Bauwhede, 2005).

External Audit function

The Lippens code does not contain specific rules about the external audit function. However, audit quality remains a very important dimension of corporate monitoring and control. As a matter of fact, the Corporate Governance Law of August 2002 and the subsequent Royal Decrees, include various auditor independence rules to safeguard audit quality. As discussed in Chapter 4, audit quality is often measured by a simple indicator variable, namely whether the auditor is a big N auditor or not.

As far as the Belgian evidence is concerned, we see that there are only subtle differences between the big four and other firms regarding audit reporting in the non-listed clients segment of the audit market. In particular, the big four audit firms do not more often (ceteris paribus) provide a non-clean audit opinion for clients that subsequently go bankrupt (Gaeremynck and Willekens, 2003; Vanstraelen, 2002). However, they are issuing more non-clean opinions than the non-big four firms for firms that subsequently go into voluntary liquidation (Gaeremynck and Willekens, 2003).

The link between auditor type and earnings management is also less apparent as compared with the international evidence. The evidence indicates that big four auditors constrain earnings management more than non-big four audit firms in the large client segment of the audit market (Vander Bauwhede, Willekens and Gaeremynck, 2003), but not in the non-listed client segment of the market (Sercu, Vander Bauwhede and Willekens, 2003; Vander Bauwhede and Willekens, 2004).

Finally, we do find a clear positive association between audit type and transparency. In particular, big four clients tend to be more transparent in that they disclose more information in their annual report regarding value drivers amongst other things (Willekens and Sercu, 2005).

CONCLUSIONS

In this book we reviewed the empirical evidence regarding the effectiveness of various building blocks of corporate governance. Good governance – in general – is supposed to serve both an entrepreneurial and monitoring role. While the board of directors clearly serves both roles, audit committees, internal and external auditing rather have a monitoring function. From the international evidence it seems that some governance mechanisms and characteristics are effective, whilst others do not seem to be (as) effective. From an entrepreneurial perspective, the international evidence indicates that small *boards* and boards in which the chairman is not the same person as the CEO tend to outperform larger boards and boards in which the chairman and the CEO is the same person. These board characteristics also lead to more or quicker dismissals of badly performing CEO's. However, there is no univocal evidence as to whether more outside directors on the board leads to better performance. With respect to the monitoring function of the board, the evidence suggests that small and independent boards are associated with less earnings management and fraud.

The international evidence is quite consistent regarding the effectiveness of *audit committees* and audit committee independence in constraining earnings management and preventing fraud. But there is hardly any evidence about the effectiveness of the *internal audit* function and internal control mechanisms. *External auditing*, on the other hand, has received considerable attention and there is plenty of evidence of differential quality of audits performed by big N auditors. It needs to be said, though, that very little is known about the tangible attributes of external audit quality and the alleged quality differentiation between auditor types. Finally, the international evidence is supportive of the argument that more corporate disclosure and transparency is better as it leads to quicker CEO turnover in distressed firms, higher stock liquidity and lower cost of capital and debt.

(Multivariate) empirical studies about the effectiveness of governance mechanisms in *Belgium* are rather scarce and therefore more work needs to be done. The findings from the Belgian studies are not always consistent with the international evidence. As far as *board* effectiveness is concerned, there is evidence that (counter to expectations) larger boards constrain earnings management better than smaller boards, and more board meetings go together with (counter to expectations) less transparency. Also, there is no evidence that the presence of non-executive board members leads to less earnings management. However, the evidence is consistent with more non-executive board members being associated with more external audit demand. Furthermore, boards where the CEO is not the chairman, are associated with more transparency about financial risk management. Also, companies that voluntarily disclosed a corporate governance charter exhibited less earnings management.

As far as *audit committees* are concerned, there is evidence that Belgian listed companies with more independent directors on their boards are more likely to voluntarily install audit committees. However, the evidence regarding audit committee effectiveness and the monitoring role of audit committees is disappointing, as there is no association between the presence of an audit committee and monitoring earnings management. There is also no association between the presence of audit committees and corporate transparency. This evidence suggests that the mere presence of an audit committee is not very effective if not sustained by other monitoring devices (such as, for example, an internal audit function).

The evidence about the effectiveness of the *internal* audit function is more encouraging. Two independent studies have indicated that the presence of an internal audit function leads to more transparency, and not only transparency about financial risk management, but also transparency regarding operational and strategic matters such as innovation and customer satisfaction.

Finally, in contrast to the international evidence, there is only weak evidence that big N audit firms exhibit superior monitoring capabilities as compared to non-big N firms in Belgian listed companies. One study found that in large listed companies there is less earnings management if the auditor is a big N auditor. A clear result, however, is that companies with a big N auditor are generally more transparent.

Overall the results of our study about the implementation and effectiveness of various governance mechanisms in Belgium, indicates that before the Lippens code was constructed, a lot of Belgian listed companies already complied with some basic rules of what (supposedly) is good governance. However, this did not lead to effective monitoring in all dimensions. There is no univocal evidence that the typical 'good board' characteristics have lead to better monitoring. Also the mere presence of audit committees did not yield effective monitoring. However, from the scarce Belgian evidence that is available, the installation of an internal audit function seems to be very effective as it clearly is associated with more corporate transparency.

REFERENCES

Gaeremynck, A. & M. Willekens. 2003. "The Endogenous Relationship between Audit-Report Type and Business Termination: Evidence on Private Firms in a Non-Litigious Environment", *Accounting and Business Research*, Vol. 33-1: 65-79.

Knechel W. R. and M. Willekens. 2004. "The Role of Risk Management and Governance in determining Audit demand". KUL research Report No. 0463.

Sercu P., Vander Bauwhede, H. en M. Willekens. 2002. "Earnings Quality in privately held firms: the roles of external audits, stakeholders and governance mechanisms", Research Report KU Leuven 0235, 29 pp.

Vander Bauwhede, H., M. Willekens en A. Gaeremynck. 2003. "Audit Quality, Public Ownership and Firms' Discretionary Accruals Management", *The International Journal of Accounting*, Vol. 38-1: 1-22.

Vander Bauwhede, H. en M. Willekens. 2004. "Evidence on (the lack of) Audit-Quality Differentiation in the Private Client Segment of the Belgian Audit Market?, *European Accounting Review*. Vol. 13-3: 501-522.

Vanstraelen, A. 2002. "Auditor economic incentives and going-concern opinions in a limited litigious continental European business environment: empirical evidence from Belgium. *Accounting and Business Research*, Vol. 32-3: 171-186.

Willekens M., Bruynseels, L. en A. Heiremans. "Corporate Governance en Risicomanagement: empirische evidentie voor België". *Accountancy & Bedrijfskunde*, Maart 2005.

Willekens, M., Vander Bauwhede, H. & A. Gaeremynck. 2004. "Voluntary Audit Committee Formation and Practices among Belgian Listed Companies". *International Journal of Auditing*. Vol. 8-3: 207-222.

Willekens, M., Gaeremynck, A., Vander Bauwhede, H. & Van de Gucht, L. 2005. The impact of internal and external governance mechanisms on the voluntary disclosure of financial and non-financial performance. KULeuven working paper.